# The Integrated Technology Classroom

# *Related Titles of Interest*

**Educator's Guide to Macintosh Applications**
Arnie H. Abrams
ISBN: 0-205-16284-3

**The Educator's Guide to HyperCard™ and HyperTalk™, Revised Edition**
George H. Culp and G. Morgan Watkins
ISBN: 0-205-16652-0

**Hyper InterActive CAI: Using HyperCard to Develop Computer-Assisted Instruction**
Peter Desberg
ISBN: 0-205-15197-3

**Teaching With Technology (Macintosh Software)**
Peter Desberg and Farah Fisher
ISBN: 0-205-16252-5

**Using Interactive Video in Education**
Penelope Semrau and Barbara A. Boyer
ISBN: 0-205-15257-0

**Creating Videos for School Use**
William J. Valmont
ISBN: 0-205-16166-9

# The Integrated Technology Classroom

## Building Self-Reliant Learners

*Joan Riedl*

**Allyn and Bacon**
Boston   London   Toronto   Sydney   Tokyo   Singapore

Copyright © 1995 by Allyn & Bacon
A Simon & Schuster Company
Needham Heights, MA 02194

**Library of Congress Cataloging-in-Publication Data**

Riedl, Joan.
    The integrated technology classroom : building self-reliant
learners / Joan Riedl.
       p.   cm.
    Includes index.
    ISBN 0-205-16157-X
    1. Educational technology--Handbooks, manuals, etc.  2. Teaching-
-Handbooks, manuals, etc.  3. Learning--Handbooks, manuals, etc.
4. Classroom management--Handbooks, manuals, etc.  I. Title.
LB1028.3.R55  1995
371.3'078--dc20                                       94-42727
                                                        CIP

Printed in the United States of America
10  9  8  7  6  5  4  3  2  1    99  98  97  96  95

*To the unsung heroes and heroines in education,*
*I dedicate this book.*

*THEY HAVE NOT GIVEN UP!*

# Contents

## *Chapter 6:  Technology Component*    **141**

# *Preface*

This book describes a teaching/learning design that allows you, the teacher, to do the seemingly impossible—engage in one-on-one teaching and learning with the 25 to 30 students in your classroom.

This design grew out of my own need, as a teacher, to find a way to teach my students meaningfully and effectively. The traditional classroom and the traditional methods of teaching are frustrating for teachers and students alike because, inevitably, learning is depersonalized. When facing a whole classroom of students, teachers cannot tailor their teaching to fit each student's unique learning habits and knowledge background. As a result, teachers often end up teaching to a hypothetical "normal" or "average" student, and the human, personal element in education is lost. For many students, personal rewards are few. The excitement of learning, with which nearly all students enter the school system, is replaced by a fear of failure or, perhaps even worse, sheer boredom.

The cry is for more and better teachers, equipment, and classrooms. One day, these all may be available. But what can teachers do *now* to improve their teaching and derive more satisfaction from their job?

## TECHNOLOGY AS A SOLUTION

My solution to this question was to take more seriously something that every teacher knows: Students generally like to learn and can learn quite effectively if they are given the opportunity to do so and the necessary guidance.

How could I nurture these inherent interests of children? The answer, for me, lies in technology. Educational technology, when used appropriately, helps both the teacher and the students to create a caring, creative community of learners. Hundreds of thousands of teachers stand perplexed before millions of dollars worth of technology. When these teachers search through the shelves to find a book that will teach them *how* to use and integrate technology in their classrooms, they don't find it. There are few books available to them that explain how technology can be used in the classroom to further the vital educational needs of today. And I am adding to this small number.

*The Integrated Technology Classroom* suggests *changes* in how you might approach teaching. Many teachers find changes unsettling—and for good reasons. First, changes take time, as you well know, and time is a valuable commodity. Second, changes involve taking risks. Third, our educational system rewards compliance and the status quo, not innovation. When I began to make changes in my classroom, I was constantly reminded of how entrenched in the system these attitudes were.

## REASONS FOR WRITING THIS BOOK

A major reason for writing this book is to reduce the amount of time, risk, and resistance that teachers must face in setting up technology in their classrooms. I am proposing a teaching/learning design that has already been debugged through extensive pilot-testing. The design is the result of much fine-tuning and experimentation in my classroom and is ready for use by you teachers who are looking for a teaching technique that really works.

The book is essentially a guided tour through my classroom. Although the methods it presents are based on sound educational theory, theory is not its focus. Instead, it is a guide for teachers who are looking for practical ways to integrate technology effectively into their classrooms.

I have designed the book to allow you to do some educational grazing—deciding which part or parts you want to examine and how extensively you want to use this design. Your choices may be based on your interests, learning design, resources, or educational needs. You can decide how to blend the methods presented here with ideas or techniques of your own that already work. You are the best judge of which areas are the most significant for you, which areas would help you the most, and the amount of time you have to invest in implementation. For example, you might start with the chapter on math stations. After reviewing the sample math-station formats, you could choose the equipment, materials, and math topics that will work best in your classroom.

The changes proposed in this book will give you more time to teach and work with each child as a whole person. The children in your classroom have an opportunity to become self-directed, to gain control over their learning, and to take pride in their achievements—as they should. An additional benefit is that the fear of failure is diminished for both you and your students. Your reward—for shaping a learning community that emphasizes caring, choices, flexibility, and life-long learning—is intellectual freshness and pride in your profession.

## A NEW TEACHING/LEARNING DESIGN

This learning design integrates technology in ways that return teachers to their roles as coaches, diagnosticians, and collaborators in learning. It offers you the opportunity and time to tailor students' learning, to provide real guidance for the students' learning efforts, and to help students develop crucial analytical and conceptual thinking skills. The design presents a multidisciplinary and theme-oriented approach to learning that helps students make connections between what they learn and the world around them.

The learning program combines three basic ingredients in varying amounts for different learning applications: (1) small-group work stations (learning stations); (2) daily, small-group, teacher-facilitated discussions; and (3) educational technology, including computers, laser disk players, and camcorders.

In too many cases, the very technology that can promote more personal, one-on-one teaching has the reputation of distancing students from teachers and adding to the impersonalization of the classroom. Consequently, I have emphasized the very real correlation between *high-tech* and *high-touch* in this learning design. The use of high-tech educational tools, in effect, allows you to spend more time addressing the needs of individual students and developing a community learning spirit. This is high touch. The underlying philosophy of this learning design is that when technology is properly used, it allows teachers to return to their students the ownership of their learning. The outcome is the blossoming of self-reliant thinkers who will know *how* to learn throughout their lives.

The teaching/learning design discussed in these chapters will allow you to more closely watch your students' progress and know when they have achieved something worthwhile. You will acquire more opportunities to do what Kenneth Blanchard recommended in *The One Minute Manager*: "Catch them doing something good!" and make sure they know about it.

## INTENDED AUDIENCE FOR THIS BOOK

This book is for action-oriented teachers who want to turn the wealth of technological equipment (purchased by well-meaning school boards and administrators, but largely either inappropriately used or unused because of a lack of training) into their powerful allies—*now*. It is for people who really believe that the future is in the hands of our children and that our best investment is in providing those children with a quality education.

## AUTHOR'S NOTE

Although this book is based on actual experiences, it is not intended to single out any specific individual. I have changed all names to protect the rights of my students. If you, the reader, have any comments on the content of this book, I am anxious to hear your viewpoints. Please write to Ms. Joan Riedl, P.O. Box 191, Clear Lake, MN 55319.

## ACKNOWLEDGMENTS

I would like to acknowledge, with special gratitude, Lavina Miller, who persuaded me to write this book. I would also like to express special appreciation to the friends who helped with the development and editing of this book: Susan Halena, Lavina Miller, Pat Jones, Ellen Josephs, and my husband, George. A special thanks to Ann Anderson, Matt Kiffemeyer, and Todd Vander Molen for their help in the final manuscript preparation. My sincere thanks also to Kim Alberg, Franklin Smith Elementary School (Blue Springs, MO), Judy Pippin, Hohokam Elementary School (Scottsdale, AZ), and Linda Grippando, Kingsley Elementary School (Naperville, IL) for their reviews of the manuscript.

Bringing a book to the point where it can be submitted to the publisher is a daunting task. Without the help, support, and encouragement from many people, this book would not be in your hands today. I would like to thank the students whom I have taught and who have also taught me a great deal; Marianne Nelson, a friend and colleague; and most of all, my husband, George, and my daughter, Elizabeth.

Finally, I would like to acknowledge Mylan Jaixen, at Allyn and Bacon, who encouraged me to keep eating those M and M's and to keep writing; Susan Hutchinson, editorial assistant at Allyn and Bacon, for her patience and expertise in guiding me through numerous book-writing processes via phone conversations; and Nancy Forsyth, editor-in-chief at Allyn and Bacon.

I wish to state here, as Alvin Toffler did in the acknowledgments from his book, *The Third Wave*, "Needless to say, I alone remain responsible for any errors that may have crept into these pages, despite our best efforts to avoid them."

# The Integrated Technology Classroom

# chapter

# 1

# A Journey through Change

This first chapter focuses on some of the less visible aspects of incorporating technology into the learning program, particularly the relationship between technology and the unseen "interiors" of the schoolroom—the attitudes and roles of classroom participants. Perhaps the best way to describe this relationship is to invite you to accompany me on a journey through change that began several years ago.

The journey begins with a visit to two classrooms. The first one is my classroom of about 10 years ago. The second one is my classroom of today. As you will see, the classrooms are strikingly different. About the only thing they have in common is me—the teacher. The journey progresses from the external appearances of the classrooms into the interiors—the attitudes and assumptions reflected by the two classroom structures—and eventually into the process of change that led from the first classroom to the second.

It is an exciting adventure, and I guarantee that when you reach the end of this chapter, you will realize, as I have, that we have at hand a tool that can vastly expand our potential as teachers and learners. Technology is that tool.

## CLASSROOM #1

Imagine that you are about to visit a classroom. You open the door rather tentatively, not wishing to be too interruptive, and look into the room. The teacher, who is standing at the front of the room, looks up and invites you to come in and take a seat. You realize that a math lesson is in progress. The teacher is telling the students that they will continue working on fractions today. As she writes the math assignment on the overhead projector, you look around the room. You count 27 students. They are sitting at individual desks, which are neatly organized into rows. All 27 students have their math books open to the same page and begin to work independently on their assignments.

On the blackboard behind the teacher is the morning schedule. All of the subjects are listed with fixed time periods:

| | |
|---|---|
| 8:05 | Pledge and Greeting |
| 8:10 | Reading: Everyone read "Under the Lilacs" |
| 9:15 | Spelling |
| 9:30 | Bathroom/Snack Break |
| 9:45 | Math |
| 10:30 | Language |
| 11:05 | Lunch |

Above the blackboard is the alphabet display for handwriting. A poster at the right-hand side of the blackboard reads, "Remember—One person only at the pencil sharpener and one student at a time at the teacher's desk." A large monthly calendar occupies an entire bulletin board, situated to the left of the blackboard. Each calendar day is systematically checked off by a student marking each date with a seasonal symbol, such as a heart for February.

The teacher walks to her desk in the back of the classroom. You turn slightly in your chair so you can follow her movements and get a better view of that area. The teacher's desk is located so that she is able to watch all of the children as they work and to notice any raised hands. Behind her desk, you see a number of shelves filled with neatly arranged books: 27 science books, 27 English books, 27 social studies books, and 27 spelling books. A filmstrip projector sits on a small table. It is the only piece of media equipment in the room, other than the overhead projector. A student raises her hand. After a nod from the teacher, the child states that she is finished with the assignment and asks what she should do next.

In general, everything seems orderly and neat. You are impressed with the teacher's obvious control over the situation. Even the institutional feel of the room is comforting. It reminds you of your own elementary school environment.

You come away from your visit convinced that learning is happening in that classroom. Why, you ask yourself, are so many educators and parents calling for educational reform? If other classrooms are as well run as the one you just visited, why change? It doesn't make sense to you.

## CLASSROOM #2

Contrast the classroom you have just left with the one you are now going to visit. This is a multiage classroom of fourth- and fifth-graders whose parents have contracted to have their child in this classroom. At the end of their first year, students and parents may choose to return for the second year.

You enter the large room and are greeted by a student who is getting something from his storage drawer near the door. Above the door, you see in large, bright pink letters the word CARING. You wonder if this is the classroom mission statement; by the end of your visit, you know it is. The students are working in small groups around the room. The teacher is sitting with six students gathered around a table. She invites you to join them and explains that this is the book-learning station, one of four "math stations" at which she provides individual and small-group assistance. The teacher then continues explaining improper fractions to the students. While she is doing this, you look around and notice that there are no desks in the room. Instead, there are six rectangular tables arranged in a U-shape with a round table in the center. The following is written on the blackboard:

MORNING PLAN

Math

Phys Ed

Above the blackboard where the alphabet was traditionally displayed, there are now, in large letters, the words CHOICES, COMMUNITY, CHANGE, COMMON SENSE, CONNECTIONS, and CONTINUITY.

The weekly plan, class notices, and a volunteers' schedule are posted by the door. The teacher's desk is hardly visible. It is placed off in a corner, and if she sat there, her back would be to the students. The back wall of the room looks like a small library. The shelves are filled with *National Geographic,* almanacs, maps, atlases, paperbacks, assorted textbooks, videotapes, and filmstrips. A rack is filled with a variety of magazines. You see a lot of media equipment, including tape recorders, a filmstrip viewer, a laser disk player, a camcorder, and six computers. All of the equipment is organized into small learning areas throughout the room.

A student introduces herself as Mary and volunteers to show you around and to introduce you to the rest of the math learning stations. She takes you to the center table, which, she explains, is part of the "seat-learning" station. There are a few students at this table taking a test, and a student called the checker, who is correcting students' math assignments. Mary explains that this table is designated the "math test and math checking area." Mary adds that their center table, when not being used for stations, has a tablecloth, flowers, and a snack basket on it. She takes you to the back of the room where a few other students are working together as they sit in white wicker chairs. Mary tells you that this is their "homey area," which is also part of the seat-learning station.

You then go with Mary to another station, called the manipulative station, at the front of the room. You see six students sitting around a table with one of the student's mothers. She is helping the students explore patterns and ratios with manipulatives. Next, Mary takes you to the fourth station—problem solving. There, six students are working together in pairs, seated at three computers with problem-solving software. They are collaborating with each other as they work.

As you leave the second classroom, you are just a little bewildered. What was really happening there? Throughout the classroom area, the atmosphere was collegial and comfortable. In contrast to the quietness and neatness of the first classroom you visited, there was an overall conversational hum and a somewhat messy "work in progress" appearance. The classroom seemed more like a real-world workplace than an elementary schoolroom. It all was just a little unsettling and jarring.

## INTERNAL EXPLORATIONS: REFLECTIONS ON APPEARANCES

These two classroom "pictures" are a study in contrasts. Not only are the external appearances of the two learning environments strikingly different but so are the assumptions that they reflect about the nature of teaching and learning. Your response to the first classroom, as a hypothetical visitor, was that "learning was happening" there. Why? Because everything was neat and orderly, and the teacher appeared to be "in charge." Many observers would have reached this conclusion. They would not realize they were unconsciously jumping to a conclusion that is not necessarily logical— that learning somehow goes hand in hand with a controlled, authoritarian classroom environment.

For the same reason, upon entering the second classroom, observers might conclude that something was amiss. The traditional classroom had disappeared, and so had its authoritarian underpinnings. The scene was unsettling because it was almost too lifelike. Life is messy—as are real work and real learning. We all know that, and yet somehow it has been considered "inappropriate" in the classroom.

At the same time, it was apparent that something wonderful was happening in Classroom #2. Students were working together collaboratively and productively. They seemed to be directing their own efforts. The students working with the problem-solving software were at a distance from the teacher, yet instead of throwing spitballs or hassling each other, they were on task. Moreover, and more importantly, they seemed to be enjoying themselves. This in itself defies our traditional assumptions about what should be happening in a classroom. That "orderliness" is a prerequisite to learning is a widely held assumption. Indeed, this concept has framed public education for nearly a century.

## *INTERNAL EXPLORATIONS: REFLECTIONS ON REALITY*

Let's look more closely at the first classroom. While it may have appeared that learning was happening in that room, what was being learned? And who was learning? What you, as the visitor, could not see was that one of the students, Tom, was having difficulty understanding fractions. He knew that if he raised his hand, the teacher would help him, but he didn't want to call attention to himself. It would be too embarrassing. So he suffered in silence, trying to appear as if he knew what he was doing.

Also unseen was Chris's sheer boredom. He knew all about fractions. He could have taught the lesson. Chris is a bright student and eager to learn, yet the teacher had no time to work personally with him on a self-paced math program.

Bridget is also a good student—when she applies herself. Although Bridget was looking at the math book and appeared to be working on the problems, she actually spent most of the math lesson daydreaming and doodling, and finished only half of the assignment. How could the teacher motivate Bridget to become more engaged in the learning process?

This was the playing field that I found myself teaching in for a number of years. There was simply no time to address the individual needs and learning habits of 27 students and to cover the required curriculum with the required textbooks at the same time. The result was that, like many other teachers in the school system, I learned to teach to the "average" student. Students who fell outside this range were either bored to the point of becoming behavior problems or academically lost.

Learning was depersonalized both for me and for the students. The institutional feel of my classroom reflected the institutional character of the learning that was taking place within it. Although it may have appeared that I was a good teacher because I efficiently controlled the classroom, in fact, I knew that I simply wasn't reaching many of the students. Increasingly, I began asking myself, How can I create a classroom that provides win/win options for everyone? This question became even more pressing as time went by. More and more children were entering my classroom with a greater diversity of needs. The mainstreaming in education simply did not allow teachers, including myself, to meet the social, emotional, and physical needs of today's children. Society was changing, but the classroom was not.

The inability of the traditional classroom to meet new needs is a pervasive problem that directly affects teachers and students every day. Our whole society is on the edge of directly experiencing—really feeling for the first time—the effects of this problem: our youth lacking the skills needed in a changing workplace. There is no reason to believe that this problem will diminish. The hue and cry is for more teachers, more equipment, and bigger schools. Yet, as children's needs continue to expand, school budgets to meet these needs are staying the same or shrinking. Losing students or letting minds atrophy in various ways for various reasons sounds bleak to all of us.

Is there a way to stop this? Is there a solution? I think there is—through technology.

## TECHNOLOGY AS A SOLUTION

Although viewed by some as just another "quick fix" coming down the pike, technology may well be a solution to today's educational challenges. When knowledgeably used and seasoned with some common sense, technology allows teachers to address the individual needs of their students as well as themselves. It also allows them to personalize education and move away from a mentality that is prevalent in our schools—"what's good for one is good for everybody." The attitude that students (and teachers) are like interchangeable parts in some machine is probably one of the most frustrating aspects of teaching for many educators, just as it is for the children.

The realization that technology had great potential as an educational ally did not come to me all at once. It was a gradual process. It began when our district established a computer lab in the early 1980s. My first response to the technology was that yet another task had been added to our already tough job as teachers: We had been delegated the poorly defined task of turning computers into usable tools for students.

However, as I began to experiment with using a "floating" computer in my classroom, I noticed that something began to happen. I observed that when my students used drill-and-practice software, they worked very hard at it. On one occasion, they even asked me if they could come in during lunchtime to work on prefixes and suffixes. Their response caused me to wonder about the potential of this machine for teaching and learning. Did we have a powerful learning tool that was being underutilized?

It was obvious that I didn't have the knowledge and skills to orchestrate what I had a hunch could be accomplished with technology. I needed retraining and I needed to learn what new educational technologies were available. I began to research and collect information on what kind of master's program was available to begin my retraining. I found a master's program called Learning and Human Development Technology in Education from the College of St. Thomas in St. Paul, Minnesota. My internship, which I designed, involved my teaching introductory computer use classes and workshops for early childhood educators. After completing my master's, I went on to design and teach a computer integration class for elementary education teachers. During this time, I also did educational computer use training and consulting work for a large computer manufacturing and software business.

It was through these experiences that I realized that I had developed a different perspective toward learning. I needed to create this integrated technology learning environment (classroom) myself. The nay-sayers who declare that education is doomed reminded me of the Little Red Hen story. I felt like that Little Red Hen. No one seemed to want to get his or her hands dirty or mess with real change.

I began to incorporate more technology into the teaching/learning process. I noticed that the more I used technology, the more self-reliant the students became, and they were *learning how to learn*. Increasingly, what had formerly been only a hunch was being replaced by a vision: Technology could be a great resource for teachers in meeting students' individual needs; it also could be a great learning tool for students. But the more I tried to incorporate technology, the more I realized the old learning structure didn't fit. Teaching to the whole group did not work. I realized that I needed to think in terms of groups rather than the whole group. The classroom had to be restructured.

## RESTRUCTURING THE CLASSROOM

The change from my traditional classroom to my classroom of today did not happen all at once. It evolved gradually over a five-year period as I integrated technology into the classroom. To help you understand how gradual and incremental this change process was—for both myself and the students—let's look at one example: the changes that took place in our daily class schedule discussion period.

At the beginning of this time period, I started my day by writing the students' daily schedule on the blackboard. The schedule was the same for everyone. The day was broken up into neat and equal fixed-time periods that the whole class had to follow. These traditional units of time ignored the reality that some learning doesn't fit nicely into a 40- or 50-minute block of time. These time periods, which in essence reflected the belief that kids have short attention spans, resulted in excessive dead time as the class made the transition from subject to subject. Yet there was never any questioning of the daily schedule. It was clearly understood that it was to be followed by everyone.

My first break from this rigid schedule occurred when I divided the class into two groups when we used the computer lab. Another break occurred when I divided the class into four groups when I went from the basal reader to a literature-based reading program. Further flexibility crept into the schedule when I assigned two students at a time, during the reading period, to "word-process" their book summary at the one computer in my classroom.

From these small changes, I observed that my students seemed to listen better and that we accomplished more. Also, student accountability for results at the computer increased.

Next, I divided the whole class into four small groups and began using four interdisciplinary (multisubject) learning stations positioned around the classroom. I soon realized that I had to eliminate the specific times on the blackboard to accommodate the block of time designated for work at the learning stations.

I felt a lot of uneasiness when implementing the learning stations, generally because my assumption was that I had to plan for every minute and keep a close eye on the students or there would be trouble. Trying something new is always risky, and for me, implementing the learning stations was especially so. What if the plan didn't work out? What would my peers think? One reason for my concern was that the kids liked the stations so much that they talked about having fun at them! It was clear to me that if people outside the classroom learned of this, they would think the children were not learning.

I also began to see the need and logic for keeping my students with me all day to provide more connections and continuity in their learning. Although our school had modular scheduling for reading and math, I successfully negotiated to keep students in my class for these subjects. The daily schedule began to have longer blocks of time for the interdisciplinary learning stations.

My next achievement was successfully arranging to have my students in my classroom over a two-year period, instead of just for one year. Over time, my classroom was totally transformed by the changes and restructuring made necessary by implementing technology into the classroom.

In later chapters, I will deal in greater detail with the learning stations and the effect of parent involvement in the learning process. For now, I want to emphasize that the transformation of my classroom involved much more than simply a physical rearrangement. It also required a significant readjustment in the "power structure" in the classroom.

## DECENTRALIZING THE POWER STRUCTURE

The most surprising part of this whole restructuring process was how it affected my attitude toward learning and teaching. Attitudes are nebulous things and hard to define. For want of a better word, I call the attitude I had toward teaching a *mindset*. The traditional classroom was all I knew. The *mindset* of that classroom was that a top-down, hierarchical power structure was not only desired but also a prerequisite to effective teaching.

Without really being conscious of it, I left this traditional mindset behind and increasingly decentralized the control over classroom activities. At the time, I don't think I really knew why I did this. Reflecting on it now, it was simply the best and most logical way to accommodate the new learning structure. One way in which this occurred was that as the students became more self-reliant and self-directed in using the technology and their overall learning, it seemed natural to solicit the students' ideas and impressions. This exchange of views was made easier by the fact that now I had established a closer relationship with the students because of small-group discussions and one-on-one discussions.

As an example of how a less authoritarian and more democratic process emerged, let's return to the daily schedule, which was undergoing radical changes during this time. At one point, one of the students suggested that we call it "Our Daily Plan" instead of "The Daily Schedule." The class agreed, so we changed it. Our planning together came about because I wanted to know if the students had a preference for learning stations in the morning or afternoon. The learning stations had, over time, come to occupy a large block of time—between one-and-a-half to two hours. Eventually, some of the students requested a weekly plan. They thought that posting a white board on the wall to the right of the classroom door would be the best spot.

We also pilot-tested a large monitor/computer combination for planning and posting Our Daily Plan. What would be the best location for the monitor? Did we want it in a permanent or temporary location? The consensus was that we could better use the floor space for other learning activities. We decided to locate the large monitor permanently in the corner above my desk. As a final change, we decided to plan and record Our Daily Plan for the next day during a short 10-minute meeting at the end of each day. This was the students' suggestion, and I found that I liked it much better, too. The overall weekly plan is used in conjunction with the daily planning.

My students know their opinions count, and we learn in a very pleasant atmosphere most of the time. I am always checking to see how we are doing, what worked, and what didn't work. Among the by-products are great conversations with my students and some nice "perks" that result from our really getting to know each other. Recently, for example, my students asked me to design the cover of their first published book of writings because they know I am always trying to get time to do "watercolors" and to draw. As friends, they wanted to give me this opportunity.

"Our Daily Plan" is one of many examples of a classroom procedure that evolved into participatory involvement for everyone. The evolution from "the schedule" to "our plan" demonstrates both the visible and invisible influence that technology has on how we do things. In effect, the incorporation of technology into the classroom has led to redefining my role as a teacher and my students' roles as learners.

## CHANGING ROLES

A natural consequence of the restructuring process was a changed view of the roles played by both the teacher and the students in the classroom. My role as the authoritarian, all-knowing teacher changed into that of a more realistic, comfortable, and approachable fellow learner. The perceived power that comes with the teacher's job description was relinquished and replaced with the earned respect of being a leader of my co-workers—the students. Rather than the "sage on the stage" role, my role became that of a "guide on the side."

During the transition from my traditional classroom to the restructured classroom, I got used to new and unfamiliar experiences, to a lack of certainty about what I was doing, and to taking risks. I let my well-defined, traditional role disappear and learned to live with ambiguity. I became less of a teacher in the traditional sense and, in many ways, became a learner right along with my students. Eventually, though, a new and fairly well-defined role as a teacher surfaced. But the word had a totally new meaning for me. As a teacher, I was no longer at the top of the traditional pyramid-shaped power structure; instead, I was one part—and a very significant part—of a decentralized, working democracy.

In my new teaching role, I had more time to spend coaching and attending to the needs of individual students. My attitude also changed. I began to think of my classroom sessions in terms of whole-group sessions or small-group lessons. Lesson plans were increasingly designed not for 27 students, but for 4 to 6 students. For the first time in my teaching career, I felt freed from the pressures of designing lesson plans and classroom activities for 27 students. I had changed from thinking in terms of an aggregate of 27 students to thinking in terms of individual personalities and small groups.

In general, my attitude toward my students became more positive, hopeful, and trusting. Most of all, I realized how important each student was in making classroom happenings a success.

I cannot emphasize too strongly that the changing attitudes and roles in my classroom came about not just because of the changes I was implementing but also because of the students' response to those changes. Their response was a vital support for me during a time of change. It encouraged me to continue in my efforts. My students saw, perhaps unconsciously and perhaps even more than I did, that they were the beneficiaries of a "win/win" option for everyone.

## THE REWARDS OF RESTRUCTURING

Many teachers find changes unsettling—and for good reasons. First, changes take time, and, as all teachers know, time is a valuable commodity. Second, changes involve risk taking. And perhaps most significantly, our educational system rewards compliance and the status quo, not innovation.

When I began to make changes in my classroom, I was constantly reminded of how entrenched in the system these attitudes were. However, the rewards of restructuring more than offset the risks and difficulties that face any teacher who tries to do something different. The best way for me to share some of the restructuring rewards is to discuss the characteristics of our classroom today. It is a conversation-rich environment that is learner centered. There is a shared decision-making process that develops students' decision-making skills and a decentralized classroom-management style that reassures the students that their input is needed.

A strong element of trust is established between teacher and student. One example of this trust is that students are allowed to use a variety of technological equipment without teacher supervision. Of course, proper training in how to use the equipment must precede this privilege, and varying amounts of teacher guidance may be needed.

Today, my students say things like, "I am going to finish that chapter tonight because I want to test tomorrow" or "May I take this home to work on it?" or "Can we keep working on this over lunch?"

Students seem to move beyond just getting work done to a *concerned interest* in getting it done correctly (getting a quality product). The fear of failure and the embarrassment of speaking up are also greatly reduced with small-group learning. To illustrate, one day, when I was conducting a small-group instructional session at one of the learning stations, we were discussing and taking notes on presentation skills. The four students at the station had just been instructed to title their notes, "Presentation Skills." I had spelled out *Presentation* and assumed that everyone could spell *skills*. Karen asked, "Would someone spell *skills* for me?" The student next to her spelled it out, and we continued with the session. I doubt very much that most 11-year-old students would have the courage to ask that question in front of a whole class.

One of my greatest rewards as a teacher is that I now have more time to observe and assess my students' learning progress. I have more time to help students develop assessment skills so that they themselves can identify and work with their learning strengths and weaknesses. I no longer have that boxed-in feeling of having to meet a rigid time schedule.

## RESTRUCTURING AND THE "NEW 3 Rs"

At the beginning of this chapter, I invited you to take a journey with me. The journey essentially took you from my traditional classroom to my classroom of today. But I want to emphasize that, unlike most voyages, the journey's destination is not another safe harbor; rather, it is a new world that is not confined to a physical place or space. It is a mental space characterized most of all by a commitment to change.

There is a widespread assumption in our educational system that what is good for one student is good for all. This assumption fails to address the highly personal and individual character of genuine learning. It also fails to address the fact that students, because they are human beings, are constantly learning, growing, and responding to the world around them, including the classroom environment.

No student is truly the same from one day to the next— nor is any one class of students the same. Each year brings new concerns on the part of students as they encounter the new challenges facing their society.

What has been lacking in our teacher training is an emphasis on the fact that change is ongoing in the classroom, even in the traditional classroom. As teachers, however, we are not trained for change. We study learning theories derived from statistical averages; we learn about teaching techniques that worked in other classrooms for the average student; we use textbooks and methods that are devised for a hypothetical average student; and we spend endless hours learning about what can or cannot take place in a given school, in a given state, at a given time. But nowhere in our training are we told what to do when we see that the techniques and methods we learned do not work for a lot of our students, and therefore for us as teachers.

We are not taught how to *change* and how to deal with the ambiguity and uncertainty that comes with change. I found that in order to implement technology in the classroom successfully, I had to commit myself to an ongoing process of change. Educational technology itself is constantly changing. And each time a new technology is incorporated into the classroom, it has an inevitable effect on the classroom structure itself, which leads to other changes. In effect, the use of technology results in a "restructuring cycle" that involves continual engagement in what I call the "new 3 Rs" of teaching: *rethinking, retraining,* and *reflecting.*

## CONCLUSION

The underlying philosophy here is that when technology is properly used, it allows teachers to return to their students the ownership of their learning. The outcome is the blossoming of self-reliant thinkers who will know *how to learn* throughout their lives.

The rest of this book gives you user-friendly, field-tested resources and step-by-step procedures to help reduce the ambiguity and frustration that I went through. The material will get you through this process of change as successfully as possible.

# 2

# How to Teach Skills and Competencies

The chapter title may sound a little overwhelming, but isn't teaching skills and competencies what teachers have *always* been asked to do? Today, we constantly hear about how we should teach skills and competencies to our students. We know that many students are graduating from high school without writing skills (unable to write a letter of application), reading skills (unable to read and comprehend instructions), basic math skills (unable to make change), and critical-thinking and problem-solving skills (unable to apply academic skills to real-world problems).

There is a host of other skills that we are being asked to add to our curricula, including computer (multimedia) skills, communication and interpersonal skills, management skills, and collaborative skills. It is true today, more than ever before, that students must be competent in these skills of management, communication, and technology in order to be prepared for an ever-changing world and workplace. These skills and competencies were among those identified by the U.S. Department of Labor in a report issued by the Secretary's Commission on Achieving Necessary Skills (SCANS) in 1992.

## SECTION I: THE SCANS REPORT

The SCANS Report was written as a result of a study undertaken to answer the question, What competencies and skills are necessary to become happy and productive citizens and workers in today's world? The Commission stated, in the summary of its findings, that "the message to us was universal: good jobs will increasingly depend on people who can put knowledge to work." The Commission concluded that to succeed in today's world, students need to achieve the competencies and skills shown in Figure 2.1.

Many of you may have read this report and perhaps agreed, in theory, that these skills and competencies must be taught to students today. As teachers, you have probably also attended seminars or workshops devoted to the need for changes in what we teach. The most pressing need we all face today, however, is not more knowledge of *what* skills and competencies are needed, but *how* to teach students these skills and competencies within the traditional classroom structure.

As we saw in Chapter 1, in searching for a solution to just this question, I undertook a journey through change that led me to the conclusion that the traditional classroom structure had to be changed if we were to effectively address the learning needs of today's students. The evolution of this new teaching/learning design thus went hand in hand with structural change in the classroom.

This chapter deals with one essential component of the new teaching/ learning design: learning stations. However, before discussing the learning stations concept, it may be useful to explore the question of how educators create a learning environment in which students can build competence.

### FIGURE 2.1   Workplace Know-How

The know-how identified by the Secretary's Commission on Achieving Necessary Skills (SCANS) consists of five competencies and a three-part foundation of skills and personal qualities needed for solid job performance.

**Workplace Competencies: Effective workers can productively use:**

*Resources:* They know how to allocate time, money, materials, space, and staff.

*Interpersonal Skills:* They can work on teams, teach others, serve customers, lead, negotiate, and work well with people from culturally diverse backgrounds.

*Information:* They can acquire and evaluate data, organize and maintain files, interpret and communicate, and use computers to process information.

*Systems:* They understand social, organizational, and technological systems; they can monitor and correct performance; and they can design or improve systems.

*Technology:* They can select equipment and tools, apply technology to specific tasks, and maintain and trouble-shoot equipment.

**Foundation Skills: Competent workers in the high-performance workplace need:**

*Basic Skills:* Reading, writing, arithmetic and mathematics, speaking and listening

*Thinking Skills:* The ability to learn, to reason, to think creatively, to make decisions, and to solve problems

*Personal Qualities:* Individual responsibility, self-esteem and self-management, sociability, and integrity

## *SECTION II: HOW CAN YOU BUILD COMPETENCY?*

A logical sequence in any learning activity involves acquiring knowledge, expanding that knowledge through practice exercises or drills, and then applying that knowledge in a broader context. Sometimes, application of knowledge involves combining it with other skills and knowledge or constructing new knowledge that is usable for the learner. Borrowing from Mortimer Adler's learning theory, I call these three steps in the learning process (or modes of learning):

1. Building a knowledge base
2. Practicing skills
3. Putting it all together

These steps, or modes, may overlap considerably. For example, the third mode (putting it all together) necessarily involves the second mode (practicing skills).

To illustrate why every step in this process is essential to developing skills and competencies, consider the following example. Assume that you want to teach a student how to drive a car. A logical place to begin is to tell the student about the basics: *Build a knowledge base* about automobiles, their various parts and functions related to driving, and the rules of the road. Modeling for your student how to drive a car is part of building knowledge.

The next step is to give the student an opportunity to drive a car: *Practice* driving skills. You start in an empty parking lot, and the student practices simple skills, such as acceleration, braking, using turn signals, judging distance, avoiding lampposts, parking, and so on.

Eventually, however, if your student is ever going to be able to drive a car competently, he or she must combine the knowledge and skills developed up to this point by driving on a public roadway. Here, the student must show, through *application,* his or her knowledge of the rules of the road (stopping at red lights, for example) and driving skills (staying in the proper lane and braking appropriately). This third step, driving on a roadway and other real-world experiences, is absolutely crucial in teaching the student how to drive.

### *Why the Traditional Classroom Structure Is Inadequate to the Task*

Developing skills and competencies within the traditional classroom structure is impossible for several reasons. First, as in the driver-training example, to achieve competent driving skills, the student required one-on-one guidance, both in the second and third steps of the learning process. Next, the student had to practice driving a real car and eventually driving the car on a real street to learn the necessary skills. In addition, the student required the teacher's guidance at nearly every moment during the practice sessions. There is simply no way that an instructor in this situation could teach driving skills simultaneously to 25 or 30 students.

Whole-group instruction could, of course, be effectively used for building a knowledge base about cars and the rules of the road. In contrast, for the other two steps in the learning process, the traditional whole-group style of teaching would be totally inadequate.

The acquisition of most skills and competencies requires using a combination of learning modes. Although the first and second learning modes often can be used in whole-group instruction, depending on the learning task, the third mode, *putting it all together,* requires downsizing to small-group interaction, one-on-one guidance, or individual opportunities to blend and apply newly acquired knowledge and skills.

For example, if you want to teach your students decision-making skills, three steps are involved. First, you need to build their *knowledge* about how decisions are made. That is, you need to teach them the steps involved in the decision-making process. This first step of the learning process can be done in the traditional classroom.

Second, the students need an opportunity to *practice* making decisions. In this practicing step, it is essential that the students receive appropriate response and guidance not only in making decisions but also in handling the potential consequences of the decisions. Practicing also can be done in whole groups by using hypothetical scenarios and guiding the students through the decision-making process.

What *cannot* be accomplished within the traditional structure, however, is the third step: applying decision-making skills to actual and meaningful choices. Think of the traditional classroom: How many meaningful, relevant choices do students have? The application of the knowledge and skills they have received in decision making takes place primarily outside the classroom, in real life, where the teacher often is unable to give effective guidance or feedback. The teacher is not there to help the student search out the consequences or draw lessons from poor decisions.

### Workshops Don't Work

We have all attended workshops that explore such topics as how to build self-esteem, how to develop critical-thinking skills, how to foster collaborative and cooperative work efforts, and how to develop computer skills. The goal of such workshops—and teacher-training programs—is for teachers to be able to teach students *how to learn* a particular topic. The problem with achieving this goal is that most teachers *themselves* have never been taught the *how* of this process. Traditional educational programs, seminars, and workshops focus on "learning in order to know" rather than "learning in order to do."

For instance, I attended a workshop that emphasized building children's self-esteem. The leader had developed a day-long agenda, with one hour dedicated to decision-making skills. The object of the session was, of course, to learn how to teach students how to make good decisions (learning in order to do). The leader opened the session by lecturing for about 20 minutes, after which we broke into small discussion groups according to numbers the leader had assigned to us. He gave instructions for small-group work by using such statements as, "Each person is to review a section and share with the group. I want all of you to do...," and other directives, including the time he had allotted to complete our discussions.

The leader did not participate in the discussions but, instead, walked around the room, observing and listening to the discussion. He periodically called our attention to the time by stating, "Ten minutes left," or "One minute to go." His only apparent function during the small-group session was that of timekeeper.

I wondered if I was the only participant who appreciated the irony of a session on decision making that allowed us no opportunity to make decisions. Most of us came to the workshop quite familiar with the *knowledge* of the decision-making process. What we needed was not more worksheets for our binders or more canned lessons to fit into our schedules, but workable, meaningful techniques for increasing and improving opportunities for student decision making in our classrooms. We needed to learn *how* to weave decision-making opportunities into our existing curriculum. What we ended with, however, was another Band-Aid to fit over the educational sore.

By using a top-down approach, the workshop leader missed an opportunity to demonstrate collaborative decision making. Like many educators, he found it easier and more comfortable to assert control than to create an open learning process because of the risk of dealing with potential disorder and ambiguity. Unfortunately, most teachers have mastered the theme of "certainty" in classroom structure because orderliness and certainty are rewarded, and also because they have not developed the ability to orchestrate the risks and rewards involved when students participate in decision making.

It became clear to me that if educators truly want students to master the skills and competencies needed in today's world, the traditional classroom's authoritarian operational mode and structure will not work. A new learning environment is required—one that connects academic learning to life in the world outside school. I developed the learning stations as the conceptual framework in order to create a real-life learning environment.

### The Learning-Station Conceptual Framework

The learning-station framework is primarily learner directed and designed to incorporate in varying degrees teacher guidance; instructional technology applications; small-group, teacher-facilitated discussions; and parent assistance.

For me, the "how" and expertise part of using stations grew with self-directed learning, sharing experiences with colleagues who were further along in this change process, and getting ideas from my students. I continued to rethink, retrain, and reflect. The result was a decentralized way of management, a more flexible time perspective, a new style of communicating with students, a focus on quality, and a better way of learning. Specifically, the use of learning stations benefits students in these ways:

1. Cooperation and collaboration are standard.
2. Technology becomes a natural tool for learning.
3. Verbalization is encouraged. Communication skills are an integral part of each learning station.
4. The outcome is the blossoming of self-reliant thinkers who will know *how* to learn throughout their lives.

Because learning stations are not fixed, they enable you to continue fine-tuning and adjusting to provide students with an environment and culture to meet today's learning needs—a quality learning environment.

### What Is a Learning Station?

A learning station consists of a carefully designed and equipped area in the classroom in which four to six students work together to accomplish a specific learning task. What the station looks like will depend on the nature of the task you are teaching. The station could consist merely of a table at which the students (and perhaps you or a parent) sit. It could be an area in which you set up one or two computers for the group of students to use. The station might be a designated area of the classroom set aside for videotaping or for watching a videotape or videodisc.

You can set up just one learning station, at which only 4 to 6 of your students work at a time, or a series of stations. In my classroom, which averages about 26 students, I use four to six learning stations each day. For about two to three hours a day, the students rotate from station to station, spending approximately 30 to 50 minutes at each station. These stations have no sequential order, so it doesn't matter where a student group begins. I use two basic types of learning stations: math stations and multisubject stations.

The math stations present students with an opportunity to learn and do math using each of the learning modes discussed previously. One station may be designed to teach basic math, such as the two-digit multiplication process. At another station, the students might focus on practicing multiplication, perhaps with an interactive software program. At the third station, students might watch a *Square One* videotape. These tapes present sound mathematical content in an interesting, meaningful, and positive way through exploratory learning, and they encourage the use of problem-solving processes by modeling.

Sometimes our class has an ongoing project at a math station—for example, making a bird feeder. Working on the project requires the students to apply the math knowledge and skills of addition, subtraction, multiplication, fractions, measurement techniques, and so on.

The multisubject stations use a combination of interdisciplinary and real-life experience approaches to learning. When using these stations, students build knowledge and practice skills appropriate to various classroom subjects (math, reading, writing, art, science, and so on) while exploring a particular topic, such as colonial history.

At one of the multisubject stations, the task might be to write a paragraph describing colonial times through an apprentice's eyes (writing skills). At another station, students might be required to use a database to obtain information about jobs in colonial times (knowledge base). Other multisubject stations may be studying art and culture (reading about and making Johnnycakes), communication skills (putting together a video news broadcast of a colonial era event, such as the Boston Tea Party), and geography (using a map program to identify the colonies and print out a map).

To guide the students through the learning stations, I provide them with a set of instructional guidelines, called *learning-station plans*.

## The Learning-Station Plan

The learning-station plan can be presented on the blackboard, the overhead, a large overhead computer monitor, or printed instructions (hard copy) handed out to station groups. The students in my classroom have varying preferences. For math stations, they like to have the learning-station plan presented on the blackboard. For the multisubject stations, they prefer to have a hard copy (one copy per small group) to take with them from station to station.

Figures 2.2 and 2.3 are examples of the students' learning-station plans for both math stations and multisubject stations. Notice that each station plan indicates what stations will be used and briefly describes what is to happen at each station. (Throughout the text, I have included samples of hard copy instructions or "station plans.")

## Designing the Plan

There is no formula for designing a learning-station plan; it can be whatever you want it to be. I like to think of each station as a mechanism that becomes an interchangeable part. With stations, the teacher is no longer just stuffing knowledge into the "student containers" but helping the student self-direct the learning process. Generally, when designing station plans, I have been guided by two fundamental considerations:

1. Does the station plan employ more than one of the three learning modes: building knowledge, practicing skills, and putting it all together?

2. Does the plan help develop skills and competencies in at least two areas?

### FIGURE 2.2  Multisubject Learning-Station Plan

**Station 1—"Broadcast News": Craftsmen, Artisans, and Tradesmen**

*Learning Mode*

Practicing skills

*Student Group Instructions*

At this station, think of how you would like to report on the apprentice system as it was in colonial times using the *Cobblestone* article. Think of the different kinds and ways of reporting. Your goal is to inform the public about the apprentice system in colonial times in a four-minute videotape production.

**Station 2—"How's It Going?": Descriptive Writing**

*Learning Mode*

Putting it all together

*Student Group Instructions*

At this station, we will be reviewing the key elements of descriptive writing and then discussing the steps involved in describing a day in the life of an artisan, tavern (inn) keeper, a 10-year-old, and so on. While you are writing, I will review everyone's descriptive writing notes in your English notebooks, so please bring them with you.

**Station 3—Computer: Technology and Map Skills**

*Learning Mode*

Building knowledge, practicing skills

*Student Group Instructions*

At this station, please work in pairs at one computer. Use the world map on the desktop and highlight the countries that make up the Middle East. If you need resource material, use whatever you think will work best for you. Print out the map, label the countries, title the map, and check the quality sample maps at this station to see if you will be putting a quality finished product into the quality finished product envelope (a standard two-pocket folder cut in half, which is posted at stations that require student-generated finished products).

**Station 4—Multimedia: Learning More about Colonial Times**

*Learning Mode*

Building knowledge

*Student Group Instructions*

Before you look at the filmstrip, review the key objectives for it. Also, read over the discussion questions and, as a group, decide which one or two questions your group will answer. Remember the standard instructions; write or key in the question and answer with a short paragraph. Check the quality finished product standards poster and put your finished work in the quality finished product envelope.

### Station 5—Experiential: Making Johnnycakes

*Learning Mode*

Practicing skills

*Student Group Instructions*

Mrs. Thomas will be assisting you in making Johnnycakes today. While you are waiting for the Johnnycakes to bake, you will have an opportunity to hear about the history of Johnnycakes. Have fun!

### Station 6—Multipurpose: Energy

*Learning Mode*

Building knowledge

*Student Group Instructions*

At this station, please continue with your group's next lesson in the Energy Unit. Check that everyone is ready to start by making sure everyone has the necessary materials. Decide on a fair way to handle the use of the remote control for operating the laser disk player. When you are finished using the laser disk for this lesson, please let me know, and I'll be in to review your lesson.

### *Are All Three Learning Modes Being Used?*

In designing the math station plan, I ask myself the following questions:

- Do the stations make the learning of basic math concepts easier?
- Do the stations allow time for the students to practice math skills (for example, addition or subtraction)?
- Do the stations provide opportunities for the students to "put it all together"? (This work is done where the teacher is usually located to facilitate the application of the third mode.)

Although it is desirable to design a station plan that uses all three modes, sometimes you may find it more appropriate to concentrate on just one or two of them. For example, if you are building students' knowledge base in math, you may focus all of the stations primarily on this learning mode.

I have found that the third mode, or step, in the learning process (putting it all together) is perhaps the most challenging in terms of station design. You want to design an activity that will allow students to apply their skills, see relationships, relate what they're learning to the world around them, and perhaps take what they've learned a step further and acquire a greater knowledge. These goals can be achieved by using both traditional tools and equipment (building a bird feeder) or multimedia tools (problem-solving software).

**FIGURE 2.3   Math Learning-Station Plan**

**Station 1—Book Learning**

*Learning Mode*

Building knowledge, practicing skills

*Student Group Instructions*

Today, please be ready to write your math goal, show it to me, and report how you are doing in the chapter you are working on.

**Station 2—Seat Learning**

*Learning Mode*

Practicing skills

*Student Group Instructions*

Take some time to think through what you need to do at this station. Check your chapter assignment plan; do you have work to do in your math text? If you are ready to test, pick up your test. Good luck. Use your time wisely!

**Station 3—Manipulative**

*Learning Mode*

Practice skills

*Student Group Instructions*

At this station, you will be watching *Square One*. The topic is surveys and percents. Remember to have the clipboards and the *Square One* activity sheet, and to use the best grammar skills you can when answering the questions. Check the quality *Square One* sample sheets before you put your *Square One* sheet in the quality finished product envelope.

**Station 4—Problem Solving**

*Learning Mode*

Putting it all together

*Student Group Instructions*

Please have your own disk to save your Logo work on. Check your Logo notes to see where you are on learning about Logo terms and procedures. Have fun!

As an example of the latter, consider a situation in which the underlying general goal is to have students discover why the math ideas that they are studying are important and how they interrelate. By the time they reach this station, the students already know that a right angle is 90 degrees and a straight line is 180 degrees. They also know what a square looks like. But observe what happens when a student, working with *LogoWriter* (a computer program described at length in Chapter 6), attempts to draw a square. The program requires that the student knows how to put together four right angles and four straight lines of equal length. It is amazing to watch a student work through this process. Although they read about right angles in their textbook and were told about right angles during whole-group instruction, most students never really "put it together" in their minds, or internalize, the relationship between right angles and squares. Through trial and error, however, they quickly learned that they could not draw a square without using 90-degree angles, and they also learned that a square has to have four equal sides.

### Do the Stations Facilitate SCANS Skills and Competencies Development?

Another important consideration in designing a learning-station plan is whether the stations promote the kinds of skills and competencies that I want the students to master (essentially, those skills and competencies outlined in the SCANS Report). After designing a learning-station plan, I review the plan specifically to identify what skills are involved in completing the tasks done at each station. Given the learning-station format, a variety of skills are usually involved in each task. Occasionally, I will redesign the plan to make sure that more than one or two skills are addressed.

To understand how skill enhancement is a natural component of the learning-station format, consider the example of the square-drawing task just discussed. When the students were drawing the squares using *Logo-Writer,* they were learning more than just math skills. During the process of forming their squares, they were also becoming more competent in the use of computer technology. They learned, for example, that by using the *LogoWriter's* "repeat" function, the next time they wanted a square, they wouldn't have to start from scratch. With one computer command, the square would appear; they would not have to spend five or more minutes redrawing it.

The drawing project also required the students to use decision-making, problem-solving, and critical-thinking skills. Furthermore, the students had an opportunity to collaborate on different strategies and approaches. The six students working at the station shared their knowledge of right angles and squares, took turns using three computers, and compared notes on their achievements. In other words, the students, while learning about square formation, were also developing their communication and collaboration skills.

### Clarity

To maximize the effectiveness of your plan, write your instructions as clearly as possible and make sure that the students can easily understand them. Remember, one point of the plan (and the learning stations themselves) is to offer your students the opportunity to direct their own learning experience. If they can't understand the plan, they will interrupt you (and others) by asking you to clarify the instructions. Also, when instructions are not clear, the students become frustrated and less motivated to do the tasks.

### *Available Resources*

How you design your learning-station plan will, of course, depend on what resources you have available. If, for example, you have a camcorder available, you might plan to have the students videotape an oral presentation at one of your stations. Or you could use the camcorder to create an instructional video for the students to use while working on a project, such as building a bird feeder. The students could refer to this video as necessary to make sure that they are following the step-by-step instructions closely, measuring properly, and generally following the required procedure for building the bird feeder. If you have a laser-disk player, you might want to have your students work with a videodisc that provides extensive subject background and thus builds a knowledge base in a given area. Videodisc players are invaluable resources for this learning mode. If you have computers and word-processing software, there are a variety of skills, particularly writing skills, that students can work on at the computer station.

Note that even if you have few technological resources, you can still set up work stations. Assume, for example, that you have a video cassette recorder (VCR), a tape recorder, and one computer. You could put each of these to use in a learning station. One group of students could be viewing a videotape on tropical rain forests. Another group of students could be preparing a radio broadcast on the deforestation of the Amazon area. A third group could be working on the computer, answering questions about the tropical rain forest, such as: What are the other issues surrounding this topic? How will decisions be made about this issue? Can you see two sides to this problem? How does deforestation of the Amazon affect you?

This group would collaborate on the answers, and members would either take turns keying in answers on the computer or elect to have just one person do this. I usually try to build in opportunities for decision making by leaving such choices up to the students. As a fourth station, you could have each group join you at a table and discuss how deforestation affects people.

When designing your learning-station plan, you also need to consider whether you will have another adult in the classroom to assist you. I often rely on the help of parent volunteers, Chapter I teachers, or community volunteers. Although many teachers are reluctant to use volunteers, I have found that, with careful selection and training, volunteers can be enormously helpful, especially in helping you train students to handle this kind of learning responsibly.

For example, a simple but necessary task is that of students behaving appropriately when viewing a videotape or filmstrip in a small group without the teacher being there. If I have a parent monitor this station and reward students for attentive behavior, they will *not* develop inappropriate habits, and they are then on the way to learning how to handle freedom responsibly. I have also observed that the students enjoy having volunteers in the classroom and look forward to their helping them at the stations.

### *Comfort*

When you are first starting to use learning stations, a primary consideration should be how you can adapt stations to fit comfortably with your teaching style and materials. If your traditional style has been teaching to large groups, you may want to start out with just one or two stations to see if you feel comfortable with downsizing to small-group instruction.

You also might want to use, as your first work-station plan, a familiar lesson plan that you have used effectively in a whole-group setting. For example, I used a lesson plan from a teacher's manual on how to write instructions for wrapping a present. I had four students work with me at a table (the learning station) on this lesson while the rest of the class worked on a worksheet. Everything about the lesson was the same as in the whole-group situation. The students brought their English books and notebooks. I introduced the lesson and pointed out how "order words" could be used to write instructions more clearly.

Next, I wrapped the present while the students watched my actions and took notes. After reviewing the steps together and discussing what they were to do (write the instructions for how to wrap a present), the students began to write. When someone finished, I was available to have the student begin the revising and editing process with me. Students were responsible for having the instructions written out and later meeting with me at the "How's it going?" station. The "How's it going?" station, described in detail in Chapter 4, is one of the core teaching and small-group discussion stations.

### *Other Considerations*

When first designing a learning-station plan, it is difficult to appreciate its potential as an educational tool. Your station plan gives you an opportunity to model the writing skills, organizational skills, and planning skills that result in a quality product. For this reason, when drafting your plan, you want to make sure that you use correct grammar, appropriate punctuation, and short, simple sentences—generally all the qualities that you emphasize when teaching writing skills.

You can also include in your plan phonetic spellings (and normal spellings too) and definitions for new or difficult words so that everyone, especially those who have difficulty reading, will understand the instructions. In this way, students increase their knowledge base and build self-esteem because the risk of failure is minimized.

Additionally, the plan also allows you to reinforce classroom expectations and help develop the students' social responsibilities. For example, you might add a reminder that the camcorder should be treated with respect, that the students should tidy up the learning station before leaving it, and that any special resources, such as a videodisc or computer software, should be put away if they are the last group to use them.

I often have students write on their station sheet the "expectation for the week," which is drawn from a list of classroom expectations, or social behavioral guidelines, with which all of the students are familiar. This incorporates an element of social awareness and responsibility into the learning experience. (See Training the Students, Lesson Three, in this chapter for further details.)

Finally, as will be discussed in the assessment section later in this chapter, I include in the learning-station plan opportunities for students to assess themselves and the stations in the following areas: their own progress in the skills being learned, the value of specific learning stations, and how well the learning-station plan served as a planning and managerial tool for them.

### Organizing and Storing Your Station Plan Files

When you create a learning-station plan, think ahead to the time when you may want to use part or all of the plan again. How will you find it? To make sure that it doesn't get lost in your file cabinet or diskette library, establish a system for titling and storing your station plans. Teacher files are usually organized by unit in given disciplines. I have found it useful to follow a similar method for storing station plans.

Storing your plans on computer diskettes and on the hard drive is a very efficient system because you can do a search on a particular topic by entering a key word such as *volcanoes*. Then, if you want to use just that part of a station plan relating to volcanoes, you can retrieve specific station plan(s) relating to that topic and insert those instructions in a different plan with a different thematic orientation.

## SECTION III: IMPLEMENTING LEARNING STATIONS

When developing the learning stations, there are three basic concerns: (1) arranging the room for learning stations, (2) availability of equipment and supplies, and (3) training the students, yourself, and volunteers for using the stations.

### Arranging the Room for Learning Stations

The major criteria for station arrangements and specific station location are:

1. Easy mobility (set-up and take-down)
2. Easy access to equipment and supplies

3. Sizing equipment and supplies to fit the small-group setting

4. Consideration of activity and conversation at the station

You want to separate quiet learning and discussion stations from other stations. There are a few basic learning-station arrangements that you may want to use when you start setting up your stations. As you use these stations, you and your students will adapt the learning-station arrangement to suit the class's learning preferences and needs.

The next concern that you need to consider is the availability of equipment and supplies.

### Availability of Equipment and Supplies

Figure 2.4 shows a math station's arrangement in our classroom. If you don't have access to tables, it is possible to arrange these stations using desks.

**FIGURE 2.4   Math-Station Arrangement in Our Classroom**

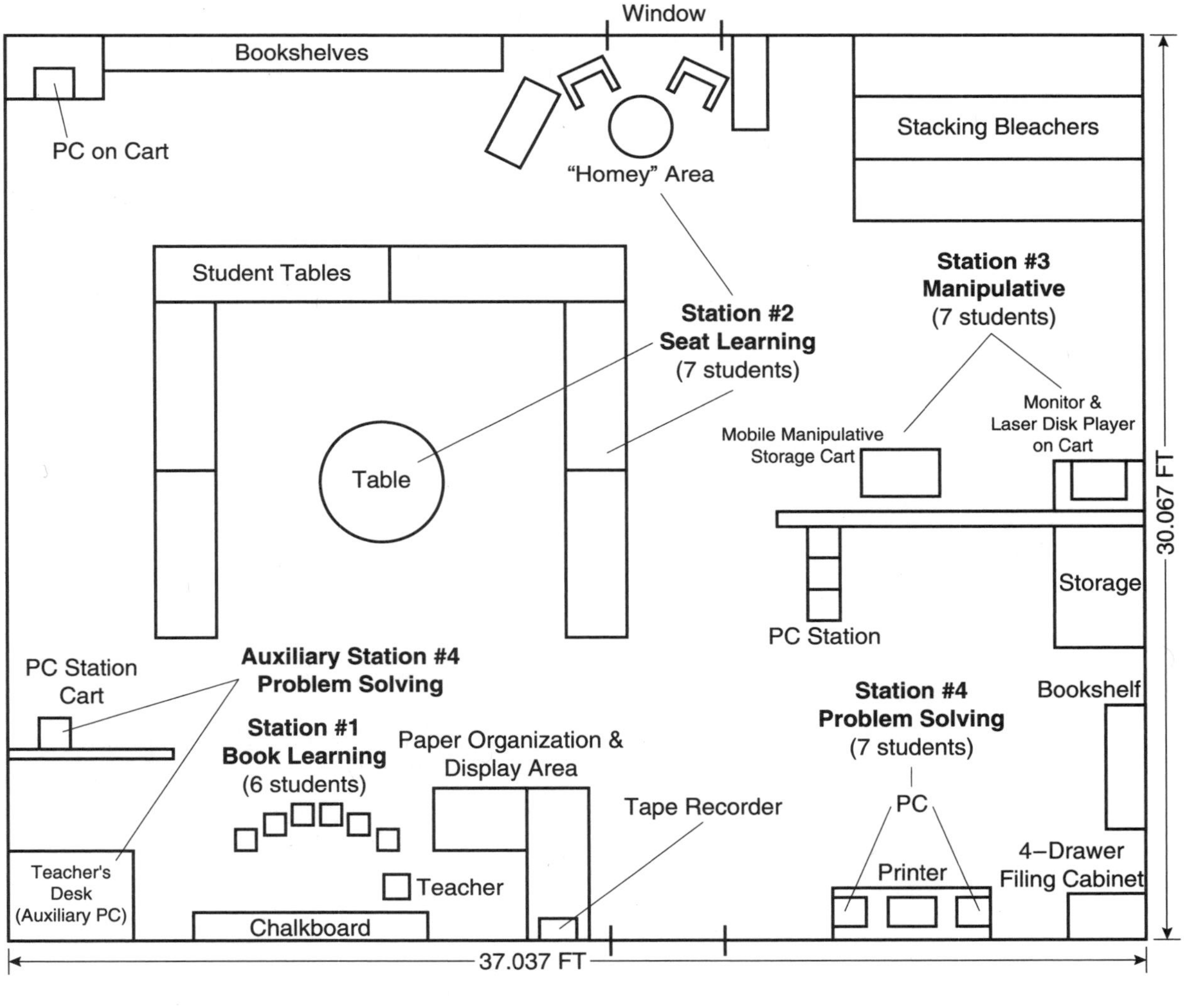

At Station 1 of the math-station plan, you need to have an area for the teacher and the students to sit at and a chalkboard for student work. This is the only required equipment for this station. Students always bring a math text, a math notebook, and a math folder to this station.

At Station 2, you need to have a table for the students to take their chapter pretests and chapter posttests and for the student who checks students' math work (math checker). The supplies that need to be on hand for the students at this station are chapter pretests and posttests, assignment sheets, and the teacher's manual for math checkers. At Station 2, students use their math text, math notebook, and learning plan for the chapter they are presently working on. They usually select a comfortable place to do their work. In my classroom, I have a designated computer available to students for practicing their math skills when they are at this station. The computer is optional equipment.

At Station 3, there is a laser disk player and *Mastering Fractions* videodiscs. However, most of the activities at this station are done without laser equipment; rather, manipulatives such as fraction games, tangrams, and hands-on project learning (e.g., making a geometric pattern pillow) are used. The equipment and supplies vary with the particular activity, but usually include a manipulative and a place to work.

At Station 4, you should have two to three computers and some math problem-solving software programs. Another option, if you have only one computer, is to have two to three students work with problem-solving software for 15 minutes while the other two or three students work together on paper-and-pencil problem-solving exercises from math learning resources, sharing ideas about how to solve the various problems and writing their ideas and conclusions. After 15 minutes, they may switch activities. Chapters 3 and 4 will address the specific station arrangements and equipment and supplies in detail.

### Training the Students

The major goal of learning-station training is to have students become responsible for their own learning. In order for this to happen, students must learn how to use and work with the learning-station plan.

The learning-station plan is one of the critical tools for using learning stations effectively. Learning to manage is a skill. Students are responsible for organizing their learning materials, using and keeping materials and equipment in good shape, and keeping track of their progress and completed learning tasks, which are called *quality finished products*. This allows the teacher to lead and focus on the larger picture—that is, to help students achieve in-depth learning and to develop the SCANS skills and competencies. Again, there is no set formula for training students to use learning stations. If you have a multiage classroom consisting of two grade levels, the students who are with you for the second year can help with training the new students.

I always have two or three second-year students in each station group so they can help the new students learn how to use the learning stations. Even with second-year students, a general principle that I keep in mind for station training is to start slowly, be thorough, and help students build a different picture of themselves as proactive learners. This section concerning training the students can be used in conjunction with the laying the groundwork stations detailed in Chapter 5.

### General Training

I have developed two practices that I use during the first month to facilitate learning-station training.

- *Practice One:* I present four introductory lessons to the whole group on how to use learning stations.

- *Practice Two:* At the book-learning station (math stations) and the "How's it going?" station (multisubject stations), I discuss the ideas of accountability and assessment and how they interrelate. Also, at these two stations, students learn about the value of assessment and different ways to assess their learning.

I use teacher-directed instruction, small-group discussion, and hands-on assessment practice for introducing students to assessment. This is discussed in further detail under Section IV: Learning Stations and Assessment later in this chapter.

### Presenting Introductory Lessons

I have titled the four student introductory lessons "All about Learning Stations," and I present the introductory lessons to the whole class. Each lesson is designed to last from 20 to 30 minutes, allowing time for questions and discussion. As an alternative, the information in each lesson could be printed for the students to read on their own, followed by a review discussion involving the teacher and the whole group.

*Lesson One: Introduction*   I begin the first introductory lesson with a videotape of a few learning-station examples to show what a learning station looks like, the number of students working at a station, the supplies and equipment used, basic learning-station set-ups, and how students move from one station to the next. This videotape is shown to the whole group and also serves as a good review for second-year students.

The important message students *must* understand is that learning stations are *not* unstructured learning time. For learning stations to work effectively, they require a high level of structure, management, organization, and accountability from both the teacher and the student.

Following the videotape presentation, the students and I review the SCANS Skills and Competencies. I give the students copies of these skills and competencies, which they keep in their Classroom Expectations and

Procedures Notebook. The SCANS skills and competencies will be referred to often, and each time students encounter them, they will understand the ideas a little better.

***Lesson Two: Learning-Station Management and Organization*** The learning-station plan, like a traditional lesson plan, is the primary managerial and organizational tool for using the learning stations. To have students become more familiar with the plan, I use an overhead projector to show a few different station plans. This allows students the opportunity to read and review different learning-station plans and ask questions about them.

After we have viewed a few station plans, I have a second-year student simulate station movements for the rest of the class to observe. The student walks to each station, points to the posted station name and number, points out the supplies and equipment, and specifies the assessment tool being used. For the first few weeks, I post station names and numbers to clearly identify where each station is located.

At the broadcast news station, students read this sign: Remember, when your group starts to videotape, let the rest of us know by posting the sign that says "TAPING." At the "How's it going?" station and the book-learning station, I post the following sign:

1. For students not at these stations: Please save your questions and comments for the teacher until later. Also, do not interrupt the teacher at these stations.

2. Remember, when you are at either of these stations, it is an important and special learning time for each one of you.

The next step is to distribute a copy of the learning-station plan to each table group. Then, as a whole-group activity, I ask a student to identify where Station 1 is located and to tell briefly what the task is at that station. I repeat this process for each of the learning stations. Throughout this exercise, the students are gaining experience matching the learning-station plan to the actual station in the room. During the first week, students practice moving from station to station, learning more about the amount of time spent at each one.

If the learning-station plan mentions equipment or supplies with which the students are not familiar, I use one of the following four methods to introduce new supplies and equipment:

1. *Demonstration to the Whole Group.* I show computer software to the whole group using a large computer monitor. For example, *Writing a Narrative* is a computer software program that introduces students to the concept of a narrative, shows how to select a point of view for writing a narrative, and demonstrates a few different approaches for writing a narrative. I begin by showing the class the *Writing a Narrative* menu. We

select and work through all the program options. When they use the program at a learning station, the students will have two resources available to them: their notes (written in their English notebook) and the software instruction booklet.

2. *Videotape.*   You may purchase a ready-made videotape, if one is available, or make your own to introduce software. For example, before using a database at a learning station, my students view a 20-minute *Using a Database* videotape by Sunburst.

3. *Station Group Trainers.*   At times, it is more efficient to demonstrate how to use new software to a small group rather than the whole group. For example, I introduce a software program to a small group made up of one student from each station group. These students then become the trainers and demonstrate the software to their group at the appropriate station.

4. *Tutorial Software.*   Students also can learn how to use a new software program by using a tutorial file: a self-tutoring lesson located on a disk. Students use the tutorial software at a learning station.

***Lesson Three: Learning-Station Expectations***   Like most teachers, I have standard classroom rules that I call "Classroom Expectations." These expectations are presented to the students at the beginning of the schoolyear and function as the guidelines for all classroom activities.

These classroom expectations become especially important when using learning stations. While students are working at these stations, various activities are happening simultaneously, and there is much more student movement than in the traditional classroom. For example, it becomes apparent that the expectation, "Respect school and personal property," must be followed when working with expensive equipment such as the camcorder. And students demonstrate the expectation, "Respect the rights of others," by not interrupting me at the "How's it going?" station.

As a reminder, the classroom expectations are posted in the room in a place where they are clearly visible to all. Each week, the students and I select a classroom expectation. One person from each station group writes down the expectation for the week on the learning-station plan. We review what the expectation for the week means and share a few examples of how we could apply it at the learning stations. At the beginning of the year, we take this procedure a step further. We review all the expectations and talk about some hypothetical learning-station examples to clarify any questions. I have found that students learn to follow the expectations sooner, use the learning stations more effectively, and eventually internalize these expectations when we use this process.

Another training procedure I use is to have the class return to the whole-group setting after completing their first station. Next, the students

**FIGURE 2.5  Learning-Station Assessment Check**

- How did things go?
- Is everything working at your station?
- Where is your group's station sheet?
- Who is responsible for taking care of the station sheet?
- Why do you need your station sheet with you?
- Who read your station group instructions?
- Did everyone have all the necessary materials for the station?
- What do you need for the next station?
- Which table group is going to Station 1, Station 2, and so on?
- What are you going to do there?
- What do you do if you are not finished when we decide to move to the next station?
- What if you finish early?
- How do you close stations?

and I do a quick station check. Figure 2.5 identifies some concerns and questions we address when doing a learning-station assessment check.

Coming back into the whole-group setting after each station movement is important to the training process. After one or two weeks, students move smoothly from one station to the next. Once these habits have been established, returning to the whole group for station checks is no longer necessary.

If discipline problems do occur, they generally happen in these first couple of weeks. For example, if the class is not following station plan procedures, all learning stations cease for the day and the class returns to the whole-group setting. The students and I discuss the problem and return to a more traditional whole-group mode of learning, such as using worksheets for the remainder of the day. The next day, when we return to the station plans, students are on their best behavior. When an individual student is having behavior problems, he or she is asked to sit next to me or go back to his or her designated whole-group seat. This, too, happens only occasionally.

These are the essentials of training students in regard to station expectations. Thorough training results in few discipline problems, very little need for policing, and effective use of learning stations. Behavior problems and wasted time can be avoided when the transition from learning stations to whole-group learning is carefully planned. The following are a few ways to help students calm down and switch gears:

1. Time stations to end around a natural break in the schoolday such as lunch or going to physical education.

2. Read to the whole group for 15 to 20 minutes.

3. Give a 5-minute snack break.

4. Before beginning learning stations, request that students have whole-group learning materials on their tables so that when they return from station work they are prepared for the transition to whole-group learning.

***Lesson Four: Assessment and Quality Standards***   The final and most important lesson covered during learning-station training is to talk about how to assess one's own learning and how to produce quality standards. Therefore, this lesson is begun by discussing the terms *quality, assessment, standards,* and *quality finished product envelope.*

A *quality finished product envelope* is a standard two-pocket folder cut in half. It is posted at stations where students put their completed work. The basic standards for a quality finished product are smooth edges on paper, neat handwriting, basic editing, an appropriate title for the work, proper capitalization and punctuation, and an overall neat presentation. If the quality of the finished product involves hands-on learning, such as a bird feeder or a videotape project, the students and I discuss how the basic quality standards apply and include criteria specific to that product. For the first month, I post a shortened version of the standards required. Students quickly learn that to produce a quality finished product, it often means revising, editing, and doing something over. This process requires self-assessment skills.

In order for students to be able to assess themselves, they must become acquainted with quality learning and behavior standards. They must also learn skills to gauge how well they are meeting these standards. I use examples of quality learning products, such as work done by previous students, in order to show quality product standards.

Accountability is built into the stations through the assessment of the quality finished product. Some examples of these are written work, audio and video productions, and hands-on learning projects. Both the teacher and the student use these products for assessment purposes.

The dividends that are derived from students developing accountability and assessment skills are well worth the effort the teacher and students invest. The students feel good when they can have some input into evaluating their work. It allows a child to maintain control and to avoid the "Tell me what to do next" and "How did I do?" syndromes. One of the most important by-products of self-assessment and quality work is that students build a sense of self-reliance, and it is self-reliance that is the essence of self-esteem.

### General Training Comments

Learning-station training goes on throughout the schoolyear, with the emphasis on students developing the personal qualities listed in the SCANS report: individual responsibility, self-esteem, self-management, sociability, and integrity.

The sooner the students show these qualities at the learning stations, the easier it is to integrate thinking skills and basic skills into the learning-station activities. Therefore, I design learning plans that present opportunities for students to master these skills and competencies early on. Of course, as my own skill for using learning stations progresses, I find myself continuously rethinking and fine-tuning the training practices. Laying the groundwork stations (detailed in Chapter 5), designed to train students to use learning stations, are one of the results of my fine-tuning learning-station practices.

### Training Yourself (the Teacher)

To make learning stations work, there are a few things you, as the teacher, need to understand about your role:

1. You become a true leader who gives direction and builds trust with your students, rather than being an authoritarian manager who gives orders from the top down.
2. Authority and responsibility for learning is shared with your students, resulting in a "culture of endeavor."
3. There is no substitute for the teacher. Technology does not usurp your role. It is your ally.

Learning stations are not the same as cooperative learning, although cooperative learning can be a *part* of learning stations. The common use of cooperative learning does not actually change the teacher's role; she or he is still controlling, managing, and policing the small cooperative groups. Your role changes when you implement learning stations. You actually take part in the learning process. You sit down at the station with the children and participate. You break down barriers of power and authority and replace them with a collegial and relaxed learning environment.

The teacher's station—either the book-learning or the "How's it going?" station—is where the trust and familiarity grow, and it is also the necessary link to students developing the "how" (higher-level skills) identified in the SCANS Report. Because you have downsized your class to learning-station groups of four to six students, you can be as innovative and creative as you want to be in solving individual students' learning problems. However, there are some general issues to consider when training yourself for using learning stations.

### Changing Your Mindset

Think back to the driver education analogy in order to picture the power shift and new balance of control that defines the teacher's role in a classroom with stations. In driver education, the teacher turns over the controls to the student, which is a bit risky. By taking the risk, the teacher shows that he or she trusts the student with a significant responsibility. However, the driving instructor does not grant total control to the student. The teacher continues to provide verbal guidance; the car is equipped with a second brake for the instructor to use; and, if necessary, the teacher can reach over to turn off the ignition.

Likewise, the teacher using learning stations exercises all his or her skills as an educator: observing, identifying problem areas, giving feedback, reinforcing desired behaviors, and assessing each student's abilities. Learning stations are the vehicle through which students are eased into driving down new avenues of learning. A teacher's role changes to accommodate students' needs in building competency. When teachers use learning stations, they are not giving up authority so much as making that authority legitimate—that is, authority that is endowed by the students, not by the system.

I have found that as a collegial atmosphere is created, students begin to exercise some control over the pace and procedures for their learning. They develop a sense of pride in their classroom, their classmates, and their teacher. In an atmosphere that allows for a comfortable interchange of ideas and information, students receive the message that they are trusted to do things right. The teacher cares enough to hold them accountable. Learning stations facilitate a shift in focus from whole group to whole person, from managing things to leading students.

### Understanding Your Changing Role

Learning stations simplify the problem of classroom management by turning many of the traditional classroom-management functions over to the students. Many of the traditional disciplinary and motivational problems largely disappear when students are working in small groups at stations. You, as the teacher, are freed from your traditional role of policing behavior.

One key benefit of the learning-station format is that you are given time to observe your students closely enough to become familiar with each child's learning needs and habits, and to assess his or her progress toward a goal. Another benefit is that you can adjust the teaching process to take into account differing abilities or skill levels.

For example, assume that students are working on setting goals at the book-learning station. Each group rotates through this station. While at this table, the students set their two-week math goals. Some students in the group manage this task very easily. Others may not. You are in a position to unobtrusively help those students having difficulties. You might have one or two students sit beside you so that you can give them one-on-one guidance in forming and writing down their goals. Some students come to this station with their goals already written and only need you to check them. With these students, you can discuss other concerns or challenges they may be facing. Then they may move on to another station.

### *Changing Your Attitude toward Group Size: Downsizing*

A starting point for me was to think of my class in terms of a number of small teaching and learning groups. Rather than a class of 28 students, I thought in terms of downsizing to small groups of about 4 to 6 students. I realized it didn't have to be *everyone* or *all* of the class learning or doing the same thing at the same time. It could be a number of small student groups doing different learning tasks aided by technologies, volunteers, teacher-guided learning or—most importantly—their own management skills to ensure accountability.

### *Grouping the Students*

For both types of learning stations, multisubject stations and math stations, I usually change student groups every two weeks. I have found that a two-week time period works very well for a variety of reasons. Students develop strategies for working with individual differences, and the students create friendships with both boys and girls whom they ordinarily might not get to know.

When necessary, you have the flexibility to vary the length of time you keep station groups together. For example, when students are working on projects, they may remain in a specific project group for as long as four weeks.

The methods that I use most frequently for putting together station groups are:

- *Assigned Numbers:* Students number off using numbers 1 through 4. Each number makes up a station group. I use this method frequently for putting together math-station groups; it is quick, easy, and it works. One immediate result is that it dispels the notion of high- and low-ability groups.

- *Specific Project:* Students sign up for a specific topic, thus each topic forms a station group.

- *Table Group:* For whole-group learning, I seat students in groups of four or five around tables, which is another easy and effective way to form station groups. Each table makes up a station group.

- *Student Choice:* Students choose a few other students with whom to work, forming a group for stations.

- *Specific Skill Lesson:* Sometimes I group students according to specific skill areas if it will influence learning effectiveness. For example, in language arts, students may have pretested on certain grammar skills; based on the results, I group students according to what skills they need to work on. Each skill makes up a station group.

The rationale for grouping students is to mirror the real world where one finds diversity in groups who must work together. The overall objective is to build a community of caring learners in the classroom.

### Changing Your Attitude about Time

The way you and your students perceive time and how you use it will change with your experience in using learning stations. Move slowly and comfortably. It's you and your students who are directing the big learning picture. Remember that, unlike the traditional classroom, learning stations are situations more like those found in the world of work. Real work does not fit into neat 50-minute periods with abrupt subject changes for each new interval. Instead, the flow is more rationally tied to the production of an idea or project.

There is a substantial reallocation of your time with the use of learning stations. You will spend much more time with on-the-spot student learning assessments and less time correcting workbooks and papers. You will spend much more time instructing, observing, assessing, and conversing with students about the process of learning and about their performance of learning tasks.

The few goals influencing how I use my time at the learning station are (1) to smoothly orchestrate the learning stations to blend efficient use of technology and classroom volunteers and (2) to multiply the teaching effect in the classroom. Meeting these goals allows me to devote my time to teaching the *how* of basic skills, thinking skills, and personal qualities identified in the SCANS Report. The small-group station format gives students the opportunity for the discussion that is needed for students to practice and then synthesize the SCANS skills.

### Changing Your Attitude about Communicating and Interacting with Students

As with changes in perceptions of time, your ideas about communicating with students will be molded by your learning-station experience. You and your students will communicate with each other, and students will communicate among themselves, in different ways.

There is a general shift from *telling* your students to *asking* your students. Instead of communicating with everyone at once, you are visiting with small groups or individuals. You will notice the change in their listening and attention spans. There is a more open exchange of ideas and preferences. This type of communication is something you ease into. What you are striving for is spontaneity and equity in all conversations. No person, including the teacher, dominates.

A technique that I use to assess my interaction with students is to audiotape myself in the following situations: introduction of a learning-station plan, discussion at a learning station, and conversation in a whole-group discussion. When I listen to the tape, I check the following areas:

- What questioning techniques I was using

- How many questions students were asking

- How many opportunities students had for input and involvement

- The degree of spontaneity in the conversations, both the students' and mine
- My overall tone, whether explanatory or commanding
- The frequency and length of responses, both the students' and mine

### Changing Your Attitude about Paperwork

Adjusting to learning stations changes your mindset about paper assignments and products from one of quantity to quality. Performance-based learning allows you to observe the proof of learning, so that you use fewer worksheets. The final goal is for students to learn the skills to assess their own work so that they can determine what needs to be done or redone to bring their work up to the quality standards that have been established.

### Helping Students Assess Themselves

It is important for students to take ownership for the task of self-assessment. This means that they learn it is not acceptable to "lose" the corrected paper. For example, I have found that a thorough review of one corrected paper or project, using group-established criteria with one or two students, has much greater value than handing back five corrected papers with no review process. The time spent going over work one-on-one or in a small group is critical in teaching the *how* of getting quality.

### Minimizing Paperwork

The following are some techniques that I use to minimize paperwork. In my class, I use 6 station plan handouts rather than 28 individual sheets of instructions. Students at the "broadcast news" station work in pairs, using 1 plan for 2 students. Therefore, instead of having 28 forms to review with 28 students, I have 14 planning forms to review.

With students' creative writing, they choose which one of three pieces they want to bring up to publishing quality and thus for my evaluation. Therefore, each of the students has had the opportunity to work on three pieces and to self-assess which one is the best, and I evaluate 28 rather than 84 papers.

### Changing Your Attitude about Volunteers

First, determine your comfort level with using volunteers. If you are not comfortable, it may be that it is just something you are not used to. If you try it, you may be surprised at how well it works. I have found, however, that training volunteers is just as important as training myself and my students.

After you have determined which stations you want volunteers to help with, you will be able to define the specific tasks they will perform and the kind of training they may need before assigned to work with children. When you're working with a new volunteer, do not arrange for a long commitment. Make your first contact short term, with a definable finish.

When working with volunteers, I keep in mind my great apprecia-tion for their services and remember that they are doing a favor for me and my class. So when volunteers send a note with their child or call me about cancellations (on the day they are to volunteer), I see this as an opportunity to model both flexibility and adaptability to changes in our learning plans.

### Finding and Training Volunteers

The basic goals of volunteer training are that volunteers understand (1) the value of learning stations and (2) that learning stations are *not* un-structured learning time.

The first step in using volunteers is finding them. I use two different methods for doing this. Most of the time, I use the Volunteer Resource Inventory (see the disk included with this book). This Volunteer Resource Inventory is given to all parents when their children enter the class or to anyone else interested in volunteering. In special cases, I send out a job description to parents, explaining a particular task with which I need help.

When a volunteer is preparing to work at learning stations for the first time, I include these items in their training: First, the volunteer and I will view a learning-station videotape. Next, we review the current learn-ing-station plans. Then, I have the student helper for the day give the volunteer a tour of the learning stations. All students are trained to communicate basic station happenings and to answer most questions that volunteers might have concerning learning stations.

Additional training techniques involve inviting volunteers (1) to view additional learning-station videotapes and/or (2) to attend a parent informational meeting. Finally, the volunteer and I determine which station would make him or her feel most comfortable and useful.

## SECTION IV: LEARNING STATIONS AND ASSESSMENT

*Assessment* is the measuring of what a student has learned by evaluating what he or she is able to produce or perform. At the learning stations, I use a combination of assessment methods, such as the student's standard-ized or multiple-choice tests, the student's portfolios, which contain his or her best work (stored either as a hard copy in an envelope or on the student's disk), and the student's performance-based learning tasks (sometimes stored on videotapes).

### Assessment Opportunities for You and Your Students

Along with changing to a multidimensional teaching and learning format, I found that I needed to change my assessment strategies. I use a combination of traditional testing and performance-based learning assessment methods.

These measurement tools allow the students and me to see not only what they know but also to observe their intelligent use of knowledge. Performance-based learning requires having students produce or perform with new knowledge integrated with previously acquired knowledge or skills. For example, to measure how much a student has learned about the concepts of force and motion, I use both a multiple-choice/fill-in-the-answer test and a performance learning task. For this performance learning task, students build a model that shows how to build for both power or speed and write a short explanation of the process. As a concluding step, a student or a volunteer videotapes his or her model and explanation.

The teaching station—whether at the book-learning station or the "How's it going?" station—is where a lot of formal and informal assessment happens. During the training stage, this station provides the opportunity for helping students learn the assessment process.

Students practice assessment skills by assessing how station training is going, whether we are using and managing the stations well, how students are feeling about the stations, and why they are feeling this way. Students use the learning-station assessment check shown in Figure 2.5 to do this.

During learning stations, some of the different formats for assessment I use are anecdotal notes and comments, progress checks with short quizzes and checklists, and student production videotapes. I can design the work at my (teacher) station so that I can take five minutes away from this station to do a one-minute observation on each student at another station. For example, I may use the technology checklist at the computer station to check each student's use of the cut-and-paste word-processing functions. The same procedure can be used to check development of the SCANS foundation skills at any station.

### *Self-Assessment as a Goal for Students' Learning*

One of the most important skills to teach children is *how* to assess their learning and then to act on that assessment. If children know how to do this, they are on automatic pilot toward learning for the rest of their lives. Students use critical thinking skills for meaningful learning when they learn self-assessment skills. It is important for students to take ownership for the task of self-assessment.

Students who progress to the realm of self-assessment have the greatest opportunities to acquire SCANS skills. For example, when four or five students and I are viewing the videotape checking for how information is presented and then sharing our observations, we are using the basic skills of listening and speaking. We are using reasoning and decision-making skills to assess the performance-based learning tasks and, last of all, we are displaying personal qualities of self-management, sociability, and integrity within our learning-station group. My experience has been that the more you involve your students in all aspects of their learning, the more commitment you get from them.

## SECTION V: LEARNING STATIONS AND SCANS

Learning stations and the nature of their composition offer you the flexibility to strategically locate yourself, your volunteers, and technology at any station. The motive for location and position of these factors is to maximize the appropriate training, coaching, and teaching to help students learn—that is, to develop the "workplace know-how" identified in the SCANS Report.

The summary of the SCANS Report identifies two areas where learning can lead to solid job performance: a three-part foundation of skills and personal qualities, and the five resulting workplace competencies. (Refer to Figure 2.1 for a breakdown of each of these skill areas.) Learning stations, if implemented properly, allow students to begin developing all these competencies. However, the most appropriate focus at the elementary and beginning middle school level is on the basic foundation skills.

### Basic Skills

Basic skills, which include reading, writing, arithmetic, mathematics, speaking, and listening, improve because the reduced number of students at a learning station raises the learning and accountability opportunities. The communication skills—reading, writing, speaking, and listening—are integral parts of each learning station, as is technology, which becomes a natural tool for building these skills.

Learning stations require all forms of communication, especially verbalization. The frequency and depth of student conversation increases with practice. This requires effective teaching and guidance that you, the teacher, provide at the two teacher stations: book-learning and "How's it going?" stations.

### Thinking Skills

Thinking skills include the ability to learn, to reason, to think creatively, to make decisions, and to solve problems. Learning stations provide a comfortable environment that encourages questioning and exploratory learning.

The small-group learning-stations environment is less threatening than the traditional classroom. There is less anxiety about not knowing something; conversely, there is more collaborative decision making. Innovative ideas are expressed more freely, students will take part in thinking out solutions to problems, and they are comfortable sharing problems and solutions that the teacher may not have noticed. For example, during one of our class meetings, someone suggested that we highlight the items discussed, so students could see them better on the large computer screen. We tried this and it worked. When students know that their ideas really count, they seem to be very enthusiastic about refining and working for quality.

### *Personal Qualities*

The personal qualities we strive to develop include individual responsibility, self-esteem, self-management, sociability, and integrity. These develop when students use learning stations. They most often develop in conjunction with the learning of basic skills or thinking skills.

The following scenario illustrates the development of some of these personal qualities and therefore why self-esteem flourishes:

> The teacher and a small group of students sit together around a table. This creates a comfortable setting that helps students feel good about themselves. At the same time, the teacher is able to take a quick check to make sure everyone has his or her ticket to learning—that is, each child believes he or she CAN learn. The teacher has time to bolster each student's self-confidence just when it is needed. By working closely with the students, the teacher usually knows what will work best with each child, whether it be humor or a quick "pick-me-up."

Learning stations build self-esteem in at least two other ways. First, with flexible grouping, labeling and ability grouping disappear. Second, the teacher has time to praise individual students and remind them to praise themselves.

Closely related to a student's self-esteem is a student's self-management skills. Students develop self-management skills simultaneously while learning basic skills at the learning stations. For example, students learn how to assess their learning, set learning goals, and learn about the parts of a newspaper through basic skills practice in reading, listening, and speaking. Learning stations build self-management skills because students take ownership of their learning and become increasingly self-directed.

In varying degrees, the personal qualities of self-esteem, self-management, honesty, and sociability develop at learning stations. Keep in mind that although most discipline problems nearly disappear after the first two months, there is one exception. It has been my experience that students with major emotional/behavioral problems have a hard time functioning at the learning stations, probably because the station structure is most like the real world. In fact, their problems seem to be magnified; it becomes very apparent that these children's personal qualities need to be worked on in a one-on-one situation, especially self-esteem and close involvement with the family. There are workable solutions to this problem, but parents, teachers, and social workers must work together to find the right solution for each child.

## SECTION VI: TIPS AND TECHNIQUES FOR LEARNING-STATION SUCCESS

Two items you might want to use the first couple months of implementing learning stations are (1) the learning-station readiness check and (2) the general learning-station tips.

### Learning-Station Readiness Check

This readiness check is a list of questions teachers may ask themselves to determine if they are ready for stations.

What does implementing one or more learning stations mean for you, the students, and parents?

What is your favorite subject to teach?

How much student movement can you tolerate?

How much noise can you stand?

Are mornings or afternoons usually better for you?

How much computer, CD-ROM, and laser disk software and hardware do you have or have access to?

Can you use your staff-development time for the self-directed learning this might involve?

What kinds of print materials do you have?

What equipment and furniture do you have in your room?

How much extra help do you have in the classroom, such as a Chapter 1 teacher, student teacher, or reliable and easy-to-work-with parent?

Do you know of another teacher with whom you could start this venture?

What kind of class do you have, and how far into the year are you?

What computer skills so you have?

Do you like computers?

How much equipment arranging and rearranging could or would you do?

What is the availability of electrical outlets or power strips in your classroom?

How technically inclined are you?

Do you have a good friend that could assist you with technology hook-ups?

How much flexibility do you have with staff development and training needs within your district?

### *General Learning-Station Tips*

Move slowly and comfortably and stay flexible! You and your students are directing the big learning picture. It is not the clock nor the confining traditional (institutional) schedule any longer!

Pace yourself so you, too, have a sense of pride in your new adventure. There is always another day.

Remember the adages: "First be strict. You can always let up, but you can never go back." "Keep it simple!" "An educated person today, is someone who knows the right questions to ask" (Boyer). Allow time to observe and to ask your students questions.

Two skills—observing and questioning—will help both you and your students become more effective learners.

Persevere. You're not only learning a new way of learning but also how to orchestrate this new way of learning.

Your life as a teacher will improve greatly and you will now have an invaluable teaching and learning resource that works.

Know why you want learning stations. Believe in it—even when it is tough going! Keep in mind that *you are directing this change!*

Be thorough when you are training yourself and your students in how to use learning stations. The training lays the foundation for building a new culture of endeavor. Make your students think and make decisions and choices. Stay flexible but focused on what you are trying to accomplish. Keep in mind that effective change is a slow and gradual process.

The next three chapters explore different types of learning stations (math, multisubject, and customized). Their purpose is to illustrate the versatility and variety the learning-station format can provide. The learning-station plans are not written in a prescriptive nature; they are only examples.

*chapter*

# 3

# Math Stations

As we saw in Chapter 2, the use of learning stations permits students to work and think at different academic levels. The four math stations I describe in this chapter are a key element in developing thinking competencies. They allow students to develop problem solving and communications skills in a comfortable, win/win learning environment.

Section I of this chapter presents the overall math program structure and goals. Section II describes each of the four math learning stations in detail. Section III examines the roles of the teacher, students, and parent volunteers, in relation to the learning stations. The chapter concludes with some suggestions on how to implement a math program using learning stations.

## SECTION I: MATH PROGRAM GOAL AND STRUCTURE

The overall goal of the math program is to enable students to:

1. Assume responsibility for learning math principles and concepts
2. Learn how these principles and concepts relate to their daily lives

Math stations provide the structure to facilitate a self-paced math program or whole-group instruction. Four conditions that are necessary to achieve "workplace know-how" as defined by the SCANS Report (discussed in Chapter 2) are:

- Collaboration
- Access to tools and resources
- Opportunity for learner ownership
- Flexible use of time

In my classroom, the students work at math stations two days out of each week. We form these stations by dividing the class into four groups, with six or seven students in each group. The grouping is determined on the basis of specific skills, assigned numbers, or student choice. Students work independently or as a group at a station, depending on the nature of the learning activities. Each station lasts about 30 minutes. Student groups rotate through all four stations during a 2½-hour period.

Each station is carefully designed to incorporate, in varying degrees, teacher guidance, instructional technology applications, small-group learning, teacher-facilitated discussions, and parent assistance. Choice, goal setting, and the math station content blend to build students' competencies in decision-making and self-reliant learning.

For example, when students become more skilled at directing their learning journey, they choose the stations at which they wish to spend more time, the stations they want to exclude, and the kind of manipulative or problem-solving activity in which they wish to engage. However, before making these decisions, students confer with the teacher.

Students also set their own math goals every two weeks. This requires them to learn how to plan their schedules and assume responsibility for their time.

## SECTION II: THE FOUR MATH STATIONS

The four math stations are named according to their function:

- The Book-Learning Station
- The Seat-Learning Station
- The Manipulative Station
- The Problem-Solving Station

I describe each of these stations in detail in the following sections.

### The Book-Learning Station

#### Station Goals
This station, along with the other stations, contributes to achieving the overall math program goal of learning mathematics in a meaningful way. A major goal of this station is to help students understand and conceptualize basic math principles. Students internalize the process, not the rote formulas. They learn the why of a computation or math operation. Other book-learning station goals are to help each student develop competencies in organization, goal setting, and gathering math resources.

#### SCANS Goals
- *Resources* (identifies, organizes, plans, and allocates resources)
- *Interpersonal* (work with others)

- *Information* (organizes and maintains information)
- *Technology* (chooses procedures, tools, or equipment, including computers and related technologies)
- *Basic Skills* (reading, writing, arithmetic/mathematics)
- *Thinking Skills* (decision making, problem solving, knowing how to learn, and reasoning)
- *Personal Qualities* (responsibility, self-esteem, self-management, integrity)

### Station Equipment and Resource Materials

Sometimes I will locate the book-learning station at my desk and use a large monitor to display the math progress spreadsheet. Other times this station is located near a blackboard where students practice math skills. These are the only extra materials and equipment necessary.

### Student Materials

Students come to this station with the following materials:

1. A math notebook (three-section spiral notebook)
2. A math folder (manila file folder)
3. A math text (I use one from the Heath Math Series)

*Math Notebook*    Each student's math notebook is divided into three sections.

1. *Math Work*, which holds all written math assignment work. The majority of these assignments are from the math text
2. *Math Writing*, which consists of math thoughts, comments, and math vocabulary
3. *Math Goals*, which contains the student's bimonthly math goals

A sample math goal sheet is shown here (see Station Happenings for a more detailed description of math goals):

| Date Written | Math Goal |
| --- | --- |
| December 6 | I will complete five pages each week. I will use the abacus for regrouping. |
| December 6 | I will complete Chapter 7 by December 20. At the manipulative station, I will use the fraction video-disc and play the fraction game, and at the problem-solving station, I will work on measuring and cutting my bird feeder. |

***Math Folder***    Each student receives a manila file folder with his or her name and a number on it. The following items are kept in each student's folder:

1. *The student's completed chapter pretests.*
2. *The student's completed chapter learning plan.*

   If students do not achieve 90 percent or better on the chapter pretest, they work with the teacher to design a learning plan for that chapter. This is done by reviewing the pretest results and identifying objectives that need to be met.

3. *The student's finished chapter posttests.* All finished chapter posttests are kept in this folder. Students take the posttest when all the work on their chapter learning plans has been completed and reviewed.

The math folders are distributed to each student during math time. At other times, they are stored in numerical order in a file cabinet for easy access for both the students and the teacher.

Folder distribution and collection can be the responsibility of one student on a bimonthly or monthly basis, or each student can retrieve his or her own folder before math time and place it back in the file cabinet when finished. I like to delegate this task to one student because it eliminates my need to monitor this routine and it helps students develop the habit of keeping all math materials in one place.

Folders do not go home without my permission. Also, to avoid losses, we have a special envelope for transporting the math folder to and from home.

***Math Text***    A standard math text is important but is only one aspect of the math program. I use the text selected by my school district, which is the *Heath Mathematics* textbook by Rucker, Dilley, and Lowry. It has the basic mathematics scope and sequence and meets the criteria for building students' knowledge base for math. Classrooms need to be math resource centers also. With this goal in mind, I keep a variety of math texts for different skill levels in the classroom to which students may refer.

### Station Happenings

I spend most of my time at the book-learning station. The primary task at this station is to build the students' math knowledge base using the traditional math text and myself as the two major resources.

The instructional method may involve one-on-one discussions with particular students or teacher-facilitated, small-group discussions. This station is rich with conversation. One of my major responsibilities is to model respect for individual learning preferences and differences, which decreases the students' fear of failure and feelings of embarrassment for "not getting it."

Learning how to use the math stations, especially the book-learning station, requires a lot of time for both the student and teacher. I continuously train and coach students to develop competency in organization and assessment skills. For example, I present an introductory lesson to the whole class on how to write math goal statements. However, at the book-learning station, each student continues his or her math-goal learning by writing and revising new math goals every two to three weeks with teacher guidance.

Continuous coaching is also required to develop each student's ability to apply reading and comprehension skills to concepts presented in the math book. Due to the relatively risk-free environment of this work station, the students freely ask questions and openly discuss their problems and concerns about basic math principles and concepts. Often, students will demonstrate to the group how they work through a problem.

Once in a while I have the option to use a parent volunteer at this station. For example, a parent who was teaching a class on goal setting for adults asked if she could help at the book-learning station to help students hone their skills in writing math goals.

### Special Benefits

One of the special benefits of the book-learning station is that you have the time to involve yourself in each student's concerns and progress. You have the time to ask "How's it going?" and the time to wait for the student's response. You have the time to watch children work and to help them solve their own problems by allowing them to figure it out. You have the time to encourage a student who needs some motivation or to add some humor to the learning environment. You can "prime the pump" to start a stream of thought or use a "shot of oil" to make a student's "brain gears" work more smoothly.

### Tailoring the Learning Process to Individual Needs

At this station, I also have an opportunity to help a student stay on task and focused. For example, after several observations of Kelly's study habits, I believe that she needs to practice staying on task. I may jokingly request that she "sit right next to me" while she is at this station or ask her to remain at this station rather than moving to the next station. In this way, I can observe whether she is staying on task and praise her when she does.

Another benefit of the book-learning station is that you are in a position to tailor the learning process to meet students' individual needs. For example, while I provide instructional assistance to a student or students, I can ask that other students who are also at this station just listen. There are several reasons for doing this. The most common one is that other students may also benefit from the explanation. For instance, I know from helping John yesterday at this station that listening to this explanation may be all he needs for the math concept to take hold.

### Bolstering Self-Confidence and Pride

This station also allows me to bolster students' self-confidence. For example, I might ask Karen to help me assist another student in learning a certain math concept. Because I work so closely with each student, I know that Karen is fully capable of teaching the concept and will be happy to have me observe her competence.

As another example, consider Manuel's situation. He has a very difficult time getting organized and bringing the necessary materials to the book-learning station. One day, he succeeds in remembering to bring his corrected pretest and chapter learning plan to the station. He can hardly wait until we are all seated to show me that he has what he is supposed to have and that he has checked off his progress on his learning plan. The six of us at this station applaud his success and request he keep this up. He beams and replies, "I'll sure try!" We have achieved a lot.

### We Are All Teachers and Learners

The book-learning station also fosters the attitude that we are all teachers and learners working together. To illustrate, Jaclyn has just expressed her frustration with decimals and place values. She shows us the page she is working on in the math book. Elizabeth plays the role of teacher when reminding Jaclyn how to read and comprehend the math book pages.

Elizabeth begins with a question: "Have you read this page?" Then she explains to Jaclyn how to study the examples in the book and reminds her, "When you are reading for information, you will have to read it two or three times. It's okay, though, 'cause it works. I know."

This is Jaclyn's first year in the program and Elizabeth's second. Training students to view the math book as something to read and comprehend, rather than as simply a collection of rows of problems to be worked, is a time-consuming task. However, it is worth the effort.

If you persevere, your life as a teacher will improve greatly. You will be able to give your students a gift that they may possess for the rest of their life: independence and confidence as learners.

### Assessment and Accountability

To a certain extent, station assessment and accountability are qualitative in nature. Intrinsic motivation to learn math and self-confidence in math achievements clearly cannot be "measured" by the traditional criteria, and yet motivation and self-confidence are among the desired goals of this math program.

Consider, for example, these students' responses: Brian tells me he stayed up until midnight last night doing his math because he "really knows it and just couldn't stop." Renee tells me that she never liked math before but now she does, and she wants to show me what she's accomplished. She is very proud of herself because, as she puts it, "I really understand fractions." She would like to know the answer to a question she has: "Why is it this way? Couldn't it be another way?" Brian's enthusiasm and Renee's desire to understand the "why" of a math principle fall outside the scope of traditional evaluation.

Part of the assessment of a student's progress is therefore based on your own observation and evaluation of each student's activities at the book-learning station.

### Primary Accountability Items

The math program's chief accountability items are the math folder and the math notebook, described previously, and the math progress spreadsheet. These three items are usually dealt with at the book-learning station.

The *math progress spreadsheet* is our electronic management and recordkeeping tool. The spreadsheet lists the students' names and includes columns for folder number, math goal, goal achievement, and textbook progress. The students' progress is entered semi-monthly. Some optional columns that I include on an as-needed basis are the number of chapter pretests and posttests completed and the accomplishments at the manipulative and problem-solving stations. The frequency with which you need to make these entries depends on the students' level of responsibility and their adjustment to pacing themselves for math learning. Students or a parent often help me with entering this information. (Student scores are not stored on the spreadsheet.)

Generally, the students and I both use this spreadsheet to keep track of individual progress and to check for overall class accomplishments. This spreadsheet also can be used as a progress report to parents. Allowing students to enter data on the spreadsheet shows them that they can *use* technology for meaningful, real-world tasks.

### Student Self-Assessment

You want students to practice assessing their own learning—to realize what they know and what they don't know. You can begin by having students work problems at this station and then asking them to assess whether they really understand what they are doing. Eventually, students work math problems from their chapter learning plans with an emphasis on asking themselves, Do I feel comfortable doing these problems? Have I mastered this specific concept? The skill of assessing one's own learning takes time. Children need to learn to trust themselves. They need to learn to recognize what they know and do not know.

### Other Assessment Strategies

Videotapes make wonderful assessment tools. In the beginning of the year, I try to have a parent videotape each of the four student groups as they rotate through the book-learning station. Usually, videotaping each group for 10 minutes is enough. These tapes serve many purposes: You can view them yourself in order to closely observe and assess the students, you can share them with each student group, or you can send them home for parents to view.

Another assessment strategy is to periodically conduct whole-group or small-group learning-station assessment checks. These reports are structured through a series of questions, such as those listed in Figure 3.1. Students use the questions to assess how the stations functioned for each group. These reports provide an opportunity for the whole class to ask questions and share observations.

### The Seat-Learning Station

#### Station Goals
The seat-learning station's goal is twofold. First, it is designed to help students develop competencies in responsible and collaborative learning; second, it is designed to teach students how to learn independently.

#### SCANS Goals
- *Resources* (identifies, organizes, and plans time, materials, and facilities)
- *Interpersonal* (teaches others new skills)
- *Basic Skills* (reading, writing, arithmetic/mathematics)
- *Thinking Skills* (decision making, problem solving, knowing how to learn)
- *Personal Qualities* (responsibility and self-management)

#### Station Equipment and Materials
Chapter pretests, posttests, and assignment sheets need to be available for the students at this station. Students may also use computer software or laser videodisc programs (at the manipulative station—see later in this chapter). Also, rulers, protractors, compasses, and other items that are located on the manipulative cart are sometimes used here.

---

**FIGURE 3.1   Sample Questions for Assessing Station Reports**

- How did you do today?
- Was everyone in the group on task and cooperative?
- Do you have any questions about a specific station?
- Did you like working at the stations?
- Compare and contrast between whole-group and station learning.
- How do you feel about learning in whole group?
- Identify an overall word that best describes you at station learning.
- Identify an overall word that best describes you at whole-group learning.
- Share which station was your favorite and tell why.
- Did you find that you really made progress at a specific station?
- Did you have any problems?
- What were they?
- How can we solve the problem?
- Did you leave the station as you found it?
- Did you make any new discoveries?

---

*Student Materials*

Students routinely use the same items they used at the book-learning station, which are their textbook, math notebook, and learning plan from their math folder. Other materials students may need are the chapter pretests and posttests and the teacher's manual for correcting.

*Station Happenings*

Three basic activities happen at the seat-learning station:

1. Students take pretests and posttests.
2. Students work on their chapter learning plans, either independently or in pairs.
3. Students have their completed math work checked at this station.

***Chapter Pretests and Posttests***    After completing the first four chapters in the math text, students are free to choose which area of the book they want to work on. Students confer with the teacher before making a final decision. After selecting a particular chapter, students take a standard comprehensive chapter pretest. If students achieve a score of 90 percent on the pretest, they can go on to try the next chapter's pretest. If a score of 90 percent is not achieved, the student and I design a chapter learning plan, and students begin the chapter work. Once the work is satisfactory, students take the chapter posttest.

Designing a chapter learning plan involves assigning work to give students practice in meeting objectives that they did not master on the pretest. To illustrate, Mary takes the Chapter 5 pretest and we design a chapter learning plan. When she has completed the Chapter 5 learning plan and has met the requirement of less than four errors on the final chapter check-up, she is ready to take the Chapter 5 posttest. She gets a Chapter 5 posttest and sits down at the center table—the designated test-taking area. Mary finishes the test and leaves it with me to be corrected. If she scores 90 percent or higher on the posttest, indicating mastery, she can move on to the next chapter and repeat the process.

All the pretests, posttests, and chapter assignment sheets (used for designing chapter learning plans) are stored in the file cabinet where the math folders are stored.

***Working on Chapter Learning Plans***    Often, especially at the beginning of the school year, I use a volunteer at the seat-learning station. Students usually find a comfortable place to sit. One of their favorite places is the "homey" area of the classroom, which has a beanbag chair and wicker chairs. Sometimes they just sit or lie on the floor.

When students establish the basic station routine, they can exercise some options to accommodate their individual learning preferences and needs. For example, Matthew has figured out he can do a certain amount of his seatwork at home, so at the book-learning station he tells me that during the seat-learning station, he would like to work on his Logo design for the next two days. (For further details about Logo, see Station Equipment and Resource Materials under the heading The Problem-Solving Station later in this chapter.) He would like to clean up some of his Logo procedures. Mathew's record for achieving his math goals for the last three months is perfect, so we decide he may do this.

As part of this station, students might review math concepts on the laser videodisc. For example, three students who are working on fractions decide they would like to use the *Mastering Fractions* videodisc to help them understand a particular concept a little better. They first check to see if anyone at the manipulative station (where the videodisc player is normally used) is using or wants to use the videodisc player. If the equipment is available, the three students will spend 15 minutes or so with the appropriate chapter on the videodisc and then begin their individual seatwork. (See Chapter 6 for further details about *Mastering Fractions* videodisc.)

***Math Checkers***    The students' math work is checked by a student "math checker" at the seat-learning station using the teacher's manual. There are four math checkers, one from each group, who have this duty for one week. On a given day, you might see this picture: Jason, the math checker for his seat-learning station group, checks the students' work while sitting at the table in the center of the room. Seated across from Jason is Ted, who is taking a pretest (all testing is done at the center table). Barbara, who is posttesting, sits next to Ted.

### Assessment and Accountability

The major items used in assessing student progress and accountability are chapter learning plans, pretests, and posttests.

## The Manipulative Station

### Station Goals

The goal of this station is to increase the students' understanding of abstract math concepts. The manipulative station provides physical objects and experiential learning materials, and hands-on building projects to accomplish this goal. These activities help students learn how to think mathematically in a concrete way.

### SCANS Goals
- *Basic Skills* (reading, writing, arithmetic/mathematics)
- *Thinking Skills* (creative thinking, problem solving, seeing things in the mind's eye, reasoning)
- *Personal Qualities* (responsibility, sociability, self-management)

### Station Equipment and Resource Materials
1. *Basic Materials:* Tangrams, counting items (such as beans, buttons, chips, muffin tins), geoboards, pattern blocks, Cuisenaire rods, dice, multiplication boards, factor and multiple cards, abacus,

graph paper, wood blocks, string, yarn, measuring cups, spoons, rulers, and protractors.

2. *Resource Books:*
   - *Math Their Way* by Marilyn Burns
   - *Mindstorms* by Seymor Papert
   - *Mathematics: A Way of Thinking* by Robert Baratta-Lorton
   - *Moving on with Geoboards* by Shirley Hoogeboom (primarily for students)
   - *Housebuilding* by Lester Walker (primarily for students)

3. *Magazines*
   - *3-2-1 Contact*
   - *Zillions*

4. *Computer and Videodisc Software:* The software that is used at this station helps the student move from a concrete to an abstract math concept. It usually has a drill-and-practice focus with extra help provided, such as an extra visual cue or an explanation to direct the student to the next step. Most software includes a feature that allows the teacher to control the number and types of problems presented and a record of student work. The students and I usually preview the software before I buy it.

5. *Videotapes:* I have found the *Square One* videotapes especially useful. *Square One* is an educational television program with a focus on math concepts. The producers encourage educators to tape their programs for educational use. These tapes meet three objectives: (1) to present sound mathematical content in an interesting, accessible, and meaningful manner by exploratory learning; (2) to encourage the use and application of problem-solving processes by modeling; and (3) to promote positive attitudes toward, and enthusiasm for, mathematics by modeling.

### Student Materials

I keep most of the materials that the students use stored on a cart at this station. The software is located on a shelf next to the computer. The videodiscs are stored on a shelf under the laser disk player. The player is also kept on a cart so that it can be moved to different locations.

### Station Happenings

At the beginning of the year, I normally select the manipulative to be used at this station. How long I continue to select the manipulatives to be used depends on the characteristics of the class. For example, at the beginning of the year, I know there are at least seven or eight students working on fractions. Also, I can be fairly sure that everyone will eventually study fractions. Based on this information, I may decide to introduce the students to some of the fraction manipulatives and their related activities. I choose four different fraction manipulatives. They are fraction concentration cards, a fraction game, a *Mastering Fractions* videodisc, and computer software for fractions.

The whole group uses a different manipulative for fractions each day at this station. The second-year students are able to introduce the different manipulatives and answer most questions that the first-year students may have.

After a while, when students are familiar with most of the manipulatives, they will begin to select a manipulative that relates to the specific math concept they are working on. In other words, students eventually decide which manipulative they would like to use.

My observations of students at the book-learning station provide a basis for selecting appropriate manipulatives for particular students. For example, if I observe that a student is having a special problem with long division, this will be a factor in determining which manipulative would be appropriate for that student.

The key is to take time to observe students and ask open-ended questions so that students can realize for themselves what learning tools are appropriate. The goal is to bring students to the point at which they will ask the question, "What do I need to help me understand?" and to answer the question themselves: "Now I see what the problem is and I need ...." The goal is not only to help the student to learn but also to help the student learn *how* to learn.

### Student Examples

We are in our third month of school, and most students now use the manipulatives that correlate with the specific math concept or skill they are working on. Maria comes to the manipulative station to better understand equivalent fractions. She asks if anyone else would like to play the fraction game that emphasizes practice with equivalent fractions. There are three who want to join her, so they begin the game.

Consider another example: A group uses an interactive fraction videodisc. They make it into a teaching-learning activity. They tape a transparency onto the monitor screen and take turns answering the questions from the videodisc by writing on the transparency. I like this activity because of the creativity and innovation students demonstrate. Students also have learned that making a picture of a division problem with Cuisenaire rods really puts some meaning into this arithmetic operation.

The major benefit of this station is that students begin to integrate other content areas, especially art and science, into their math learning. Thus, math becomes more meaningful, and many times students become their own problem solvers. For example, Lego experiments draw on students' science knowledge as well as their knowledge of math. When Andrea and Colleen were working with gear ratios, they saw the connection between fractions and ratios. They made up a chart to explain how ratios, fractions, and proportions are the same. They used the Lego gears as the manipulative to illustrate the concept to the whole class. We now use this chart on the manipulative cart as a resource material.

### Assessment and Accountability

The manipulative station's accountability and assessment are based on students' achievement of specific tasks, such as how students perform basic computations, book problems, or particular applications of math concepts. Assessment is also based on the students' visible station "work in progress," as well as on their ability to assess on their own what they need to help them understand a particular problem or concept.

Again, teacher observations are important to the accountability process at this station. Sometimes, certain students may need regular accountability checks. I usually handle such checks on an individual, private basis.

## The Problem-Solving Station

### Station Goals

Specifically, the problem-solving station helps students to practice problem solving and to apply basic mathematics skills to meaningful, real-world situations. The ultimate goal of this station is to equip students with some creative problem-solving skills that will help them to confidently handle change and new situations.

### SCANS Goals

- *Resources* (identifies, organizes, plans, and allocates resources)
- *Interpersonal* (participates as member of a team, exercises leadership)
- *Information* (acquires and uses information)
- *Technology* (works with a variety of technologies)
- *Basic Skills* (reading, writing, arithmetic/mathematics)
- *Thinking Skills* (creative thinking, decision making, problem solving, reasoning)
- *Personal Qualities* (responsibility, sociability)

### Station Equipment and Resource Materials

A variety of types of equipment and materials are used at the problem-solving station. Determining what to use provides another opportunity for both your students and you to exercise some creativity. On the disk that accompanies this book, I have listed computer software that can be used at this station. The basic equipment used at this station includes one or more computers and a VCR.

### Student Materials

Students bring their math notebooks and pencils to the station to record insights about the learning they are doing, and to write out calculations and so forth. This written work is periodically shared with me or the whole group.

### Station Happenings

At the problem-solving station, students use, apply, and integrate math skills across the curriculum and see how math relates to the real world.

The station enhances the objectives of the manipulative station and provides an interactive thinking experience that allows the children to pace themselves while exploring and developing problem-solving strategies and thinking processes. This station can help students make the bridge from the concrete to the abstract. It builds on the application, synthesis, and evaluation part of their learning. At this station, the two learning resources that students use most often are *LogoWriter* (or Logo) and *Square One* videotapes. These videotapes are used in two ways. Students view the *Square One* videotape accompanied by a set of teacher-designed questions that each student or pair of students answers or they view the *Square One* videotape and formulate their own set of questions. See Figure 3.2.

### Student Examples

Bob and Ian, both second-year students in this program, often use Logo at this station. Logo is a programming language with word-processing capabilities that make it possible to create a problem-solving environment for many math concepts, as well as other areas of learning.

As first-year students, Bob and Ian learned the basics of Logo through teacher-led instruction. These sessions lasted 45 minutes and occurred once a week for about the first 9 to 12 weeks of the school year. Figure 3.3 illustrates a sample Logo planning sheet that the students are required to use. During these sessions, students work in pairs, sharing Logo planning sheets and a Logo disc. By midyear, most students want their own Logo disc and planning sheet, but they continue to collaborate in pairs when working with Logo. In their second year, students do their Logo planning in the math-writing part of their notebooks on an optional basis.

Logo encourages student creativity. It can be used for developing an understanding of the fundamental concepts in mathematics, especially geometry and measurement concepts, spatial concepts, and logical thinking.

At this station, it is common for students to learn on their own how to solve problems and discover solutions and—best of all—enjoy it. For example, Andrea and Katie are very interested in architecture. They have made numerous floorplans using graph paper. However, when they examine McDraw, a computer drawing program, they are inspired. They have found a better tool to perfect their floorplans. Figure 3.4, which shows the design of our classroom, was made by these two girls.

Another example is Megan, who came to me saying excitedly, "Come and see what I made!" She had used Logo to design a procedure called "heart." She typed in the word *heart*, and a drawing of a heart appeared on the computer screen. I said, "Great!" and asked to examine her written procedure. Her programming was precise and free of any

**FIGURE 3.2    #304** *Square One* **Question Sheet (to be used with #304** *Square One* **session on videotape)**

**An Interview with Rene Descartes**
1. Rene Descartes is well known as a _____ and a _____.
2. He was born in the country of _____.
3. He was born in the year of _____.
4 Rene Descartes developed Cartesian coordinates. List a few examples of how we use Cartesian coordinates.

    _____
    _____
    _____
    _____

5. The Cartesian coordinates on this grid are: _____, _____.
6. We can organize information with graphs.      yes    no
7. $-4 + 4 =$ ___
8. If you divide zero (0) sea biscuits among four people, how many sea biscuits will each person get?_____
9. If you divide any number by zero, you always get zero as your answer.
       yes    no
10. What is the estimated percent shown on the thermometer on the videotape? _____

**Place Value**
11. Play the game. The object of the game is to get the largest five-digit ODD number.

    | | | | | |
    |---|---|---|---|---|

    Who in your group had the largest number? _____
12. Write one problem-solving hint given on *Square One* today.

**Mathnet Topic—Earthquakes**
Take notes on anything you found interesting or that was new information.

**Interesting Words, Places, People, and Dates**

| | | |
|---|---|---|
| interview | 347 B.C. | Rene Descartes |
| seismograph | deceased | coordinates |

extra "garbage" or "sloppy commands." I expressed my approval and challenged her to use this procedure to create seven hearts on the screen. Her enthusiasm was wonderful to see as she began to work on this task.

An example of how students apply technology and problem-solving skills to real-world situations has to do with our class business enterprise, which is making and selling decorative cans. The business's financial work is generally handled at the problem-solving station. On one occasion, the students suggested that it would be better to use a spreadsheet file, rather than the word-processing file, previously used, to record our decorative

**FIGURE 3.3   Sample Logo Planning Sheet**

Logo Journal
Name_____          Date_____

What I want to do:

What I did:

What I learned:

can inventory. Figure 3.5 shows the spreadsheet we created for the decorative can inventory.

On another occasion, the students suggested that we display the inventory as a pie chart, using the chart-making capabilities of the spreadsheet file. The students then created the chart shown in Figure 3.6. The business continued to become more sophisticated as the students thought

**FIGURE 3.4  Classroom Design**

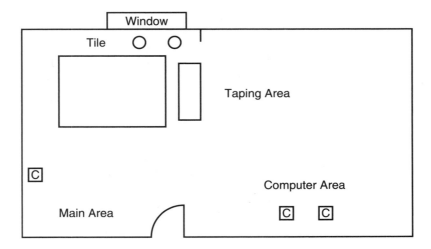

of new ways to handle various apsects of the enterprise. (See more details on decorative cans in Chapter 7.)

### *Assessment and Accountability*
The most valuable learning outcome for the problem-solving station is the ease and comfort with which students eventually demonstrate and apply problem-solving skills and strategies to math and other subject areas.

**FIGURE 3.5  Decorative Cans Inventory**

| Title | Number of Large Cans | Number of Small Cans |
|---|---|---|
| Bunny | 2 | 2 |
| Peace | 1 | 2 |
| Welcome | 1 | 2 |
| Horse | 2 | 2 |
| Cats | 2 | 2 |
| Star | 1 | 2 |
| Kite/Hearts | 2 | 2 |
| Dog | 2 | 2 |
| Clown | 1 | 2 |
| Welcome/House | 4 | 2 |
| Heart Balloons | 1 | 2 |
| Butterfly/Heart Balloon | 1 | 2 |
| Butterfly | 2 | 2 |
| Bears and Hearts | 3 | 2 |
| Flower Design | 1 | 2 |
| Pineapple | 4 | 2 |

**FIGURE 3.6    Pie Chart of Decorative Cans Inventory**

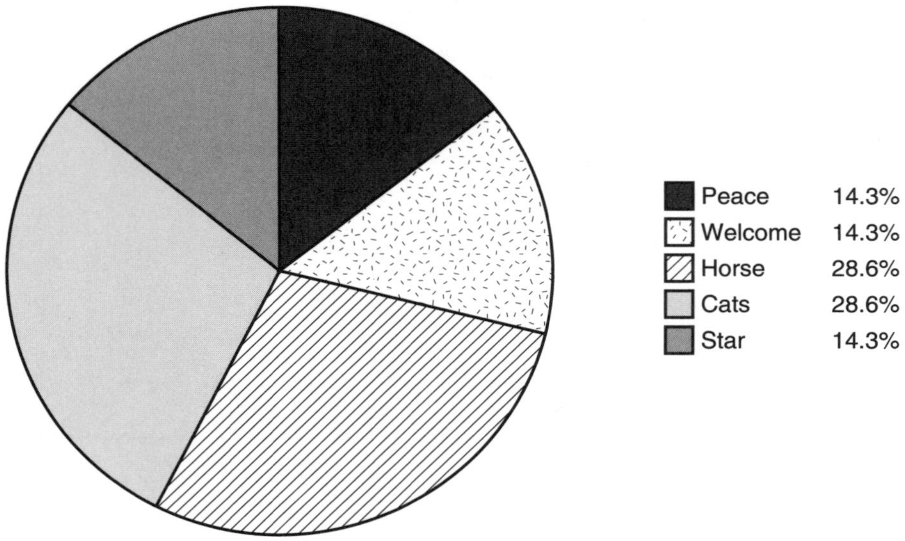

| | | |
|---|---|---|
| ■ | Peace | 14.3% |
| ⬚ | Welcome | 14.3% |
| ▨ | Horse | 28.6% |
| ▢ | Cats | 28.6% |
| ▨ | Star | 14.3% |

The computer, along with "problem-solving" software, is a valuable tool for helping this to happen. To a great extent, teacher observation of the students' ability to apply problem-solving skills provides the basis for station assessment and accountability. For short-term "accountability measurement," I can obtain examples of the students' work at this station. To do this, I look at the students' *LogoWriter* work and their *Square One* activity sheets.

## SECTION III: INDICATIONS OF CHANGE IN THE LEARNING CULTURE

### Students' Roles at Math Stations

Students become active participants in tailoring their math program to fit their learning habits and needs. In the process, they use technology, practice communication skills, and improve decision-making techniques. The math learning stations allow the students to engage in the kinds of processes described in the following sections, all of which help them to develop life-long learning skills.

### Thinking about Learning

When working with students individually or in small groups, it is easy to encourage students to "think about learning." For example, Annette and Sheila were learning about symmetry. They did not understand, however, why a parallelogram has no lines of symmetry. They asked me what I thought and if the book could be wrong. Greatest of all, they wanted to make a parallelogram and see for themselves. I approved, and a few minutes later they came back to me with rather sheepish grins and said the book was right. I asked them if they would share this learning event with the rest of the class. They did, and then I asked them to videotape this symmetry lesson to be used as a resource.

Later, I took the tape home and evaluated it, primarily as a math lesson, but also for communication skills. On the following day, I reviewed my evaluation notes with the girls, and then we discussed ways to improve the message in their lesson. They then retaped the lesson. I again evaluated it, discussed the results with the girls, and queried whether they could make the tape even better. They taped the lesson again, and the result far exceeded the original criteria for a high-quality presentation.

### Reflecting on Learning Strengths and Weaknesses

The math program presents students with an opportunity to reflect on their learning strengths and weaknesses. For example, Phillip is very anxious about not appearing ignorant and wants desperately to be at the "appropriate" grade level in math. Before entering my class, he had been in the "low math" group. Phillip knows he has a lot of catching up to do. We decided together that he should go back and find his comfort level in math.

My job is to ask Phillip quite often how he feels about his math work and remind him of the progress he has made—however small it may be. I humor him quite often about how much more relaxed he seems to be and how happy I am about this. Now he doesn't have to use up all his energy being anxious; he has more energy and time to do math. We talk about ways to make the going a little easier.

First, I ask him to focus on feeling comfortable and to remember what a powerful strength his dedicated effort is. Second, in his math goal, Phillip and I have identified the specific manipulative, followed by specific computer or video disc software, that he will use to build better understanding and faster achievement in his math learning. Phillip is a good example of the importance of building self-confidence first. He has to believe he can do it and be very realistic about assessing what he knows and does not know. In the meantime, in the context of his math studies, he is practicing decision making, communication, and technology skills that will serve him well in all areas of study.

### Developing and Revising a Continuous and Workable Learning Plan

The student and teacher negotiate and decide together what the student's math learning plan will be. For example, part of the student's learning plan is writing math goals. Basically, the students are required to write what they are going to accomplish and when. When they do this, they have to consider what resource materials will work best for them in mastering specific math concepts, how much time they are going to need outside of class, and to what extent they have to break down tasks in order to meet their goal every two weeks. The point at which students are able to create their own math goals without a great deal of teacher assistance varies from student to student.

### The Teacher's Role at the Math Stations

Because of the work-station format, your role as a teacher evolves into more of a caring, confident, and helpful consultant/colleague/teacher and less of a resident technician/"police person-teacher." To a great extent, your new role is defined by your new functions in the math station context. Rather than teaching in a traditional style, you become an "orchestrator" of learning. You also act as a diagnostician of students' needs, as well as a coach and trainer in helping them achieve their math goals. These functions are carried out most often at the book-learning station.

For example, at the book-learning station, I observed that Clark was having a difficult time with division problems. We worked a few problems together, and I asked him a few questions to better diagnose his needs. Soon, it became clear that although he understood the basic division concept, he needed *guided practice* in the sequence of division steps to establish the firm understanding that would yield the "I know I know it" outcome.

I prescribed *Quotient Quest*—a drill-and-practice computer disc by MECC. (Your school may have comparable software that may work just as well.) It will give him that tutor-like guidance he needs and will enable him to monitor his work and avoid developing inaccurate conceptions. He knows this work is to be done while at the manipulative station. He may work on this by himself or with someone. Again, in situations like this, you as the teacher have the final say—you are the key orchestrator of the classroom learning experiences.

The teacher's role as a coach and trainer is also very apparent at the book-learning station. When we use stations at the beginning of the year, I spend a lot of time teaching and coaching students about how to identify math concepts they don't understand.

I find that assessing my own station comfort level is a good way for me to tell how well I am fulfilling each of these functions. For example, if I find that I do not have the time to both *observe* and *discuss* each individual student's math learning process, I need to step back and see what the problem is and then fix it.

### The Volunteer's Role at the Math Stations

The volunteer's (usually a parent) primary role at stations is helping the teacher perform his or her roles and functions better. Some of the tasks that volunteers perform are assisting students at the seat-learning station, helping students enter their math goals on the spreadsheet, and working at the manipulative station.

A crucial factor in making effective use of volunteers is how thoroughly they are trained and understand the overall math program objectives, as well as the specific station tasks. Volunteers need to understand their role at the station and the students' station tasks. (See Training Volunteers in Chapter 2.)

A basic part of training volunteers to work at math stations involves my modeling what I want to happen at the manipulative or seat-learning stations. These are the two stations where volunteers most often work. By assisting at the learning stations, parents show support for their children's education and actively invest in their future.

## SECTION IV: IMPLEMENTATION OF MATH STATIONS

When implementing math stations, there are two basic concerns: arranging the room for math stations and training the students in how to use the stations.

### Arranging the Room for Math Stations

The stations are set up to provide both easy access to learning materials and a comfortable, interactive learning environment. Generally, when setting up stations, two things to keep in mind are that (1) a station should be situated to minimize the noise and (2) a station should be located within easy access to materials and equipment.

There are a few specific considerations to keep in mind for the manipulative or problem-solving stations when they involve use of a VCR, videodisc, or camcorder. Select an area where these activities will not interfere with another station. Also, once station routines are established, both the manipulative station and the problem-solving station may be set up so that students from both stations share a set of computers.

### Initial Student-Training Procedure

Chapter 2 outlined basic learning-station training procedures. The following discussion focuses on training procedures specific to math stations.

To introduce the math stations, I use the overhead projector or the blackboard to introduce the *math-station plan*, which identifies each of the four math stations. I describe specifically the goals, learning activities, and responsibilities at each station.

While still displaying the math-station plan, I have a second-year student simulate station movements for the rest of the class. (If students are in their first year of implementation, the teacher models the behavior.) The student walks to each station, points out the posted station name and activities for the day, and shows what materials are needed at each station. For example, at the manipulative station, he points to the manipulatives' cart and the manipulative to be used that day. He also points out the accountability technique being used at each station. At the manipulative station, for example, students show their finished task or product to the volunteer and then check themselves off on the recordkeeping sheet.

I devote a lot of time to instructing students in how to operate stations. To accomplish this, I repeat these procedures as needed.

### Keep It Simple at First

When I begin using stations, I concentrate on keeping things *simple*. To introduce math stations into your classroom, you may want to begin with only one station. This station could include a group of four to five students working with you at a specific task. You can have the rest of the class working on math individually at their seats. When you feel ready, you can add another station.

Another option for keeping it simple in the beginning is to have students work on the same math concept at all four stations. For example, you might decide to use geometry as the concept and then relate all stations activities to geometry. See Figure 3.7.

### Take Time to Evaluate Changing Learning Perspectives

As you begin to use math stations, you will notice how using stations affects traditional classroom relationships and the learning culture. Together, you and your students are forming a learning *perspective* (attitude) that is quite different from traditional math learning.

You want to take time to reflect on how this perspective is developing. As students begin to use the stations, you and your students might spend 20 to 30 minutes at the end of the math session to share station happenings as a whole class or by station groups, and generally evaluate the development of this new learning perspective.

You might use some of the questions listed in Figure 3.1 or Figure 2.5 in the previous chapter to elicit student reports and discussions of their experiences with the stations. You, as the teacher, can share your observations with the students as well.

### Mini-Competency Math Lessons

At the beginning of the year, as part of the students' training, I set aside about one hour each Friday for small-group, mini-competency math lessons. These lessons last approximately 20 minutes and contain instruction on two or three math concepts in which students feel they need additional help. These lessons are a way to further accommodate students'

**FIGURE 3.7    Math Stations: Learning Plan Sample**

**Student Group Instructions**

*Station 1: Book-Learning Station*
Today, be ready to share with me your successes, problems, and questions you may have about your geometry work. Please remember to bring your geometry chapter learning plan.

*Station 2: Seat-Learning Station*
Take some time to think through what you need to do at this station. Check your geometry chapter learning plan. You are a great and dedicated learner.

*Station 3: Manipulative Station*
At this station, there are geoboards and geoboard activities. Check which activity you are on. When you complete a geoboard activity, sketch it in your notebook. Please show both your notebook and geoboard activity to Ms. Ames and check yourself off.

*Station 4: Problem-Solving Station*
Please use *LogoWriter* or *McDraw* to replicate a few of the geoboard shapes you made at the manipulative station. Allow enough time to print out your work and place this in the quality finished product envelope. If you have some extra time at this station, please investigate "MORE Geoboard Puzzle" learning from the *3-2-1 Contact* magazines on the center table. Enjoy yourselves!

different learning needs as well as to help students begin to think about their own learning habits. After the first two months, I can phase these mini-lessons out or use them when needed.

I determine the concepts to be dealt with in the mini-competency lessons from my observations and work with individual students at the book-learning station. I post a sign-up sheet that lists the concepts that will be covered in Friday's mini-lesson. For example, the list of concepts for this Friday might be as follows:

1. Equivalent fractions

2. Improper fractions and mixed numbers

3. Least common multiples

Students sign up for one of the lessons by Thursday afternoon if they think they need additional help. This sign-up procedure is another opportunity for students to think about their own learning.

Although students voluntarily sign up for these lessons, you, as the teacher, have the last word on this. For example, I allow two weeks for students to voluntarily sign up for these lessons. If there is a student during those two weeks who I believe should have signed up but has not done so, I discuss the situation with him or her.

### Math Progress Checks

Another checkpoint that I use at the beginning of the year is a weekly check to see what math progress the students have made during the week. I allow about 30 minutes on Friday morning for this activity. During this time, I have the students bring me their chapter learning plans and their math notebooks. We check to see what they have accomplished and how it compares with their math goals. Eventually, this progress check is only necessary on an occasional basis. The progress check becomes a function of the book-learning station operation.

There are other ways in which you can customize the stations to accommodate your needs as well as your students' needs. For example, you might want to change the length of time students work at the stations or the days on which you have them. One option is to have math stations on a daily basis for a shorter period of time. Also, some of your students might conclude on a particular day that they do not need any help at the book-learning station. They may ask you if they can skip this station and continue working on a project they've begun at the problem-solving station instead. Your answer will depend on the individual students and their past record of performance. The stations are designed to encourage a variety of requests such as this one and to accommodate these circumstances.

You will get a feel for what works best for you and your students after you have worked with the stations for a while. Again, take time to do some reflective thinking or "station journaling" by yourself and with your whole class to know what is and is not working. This will allow you to effectively engage in the restructuring of the work cycle when using math stations. Rethink, retrain, and reflect.

# 4

# Multisubject Stations: The Learning Continuum

In Chapter 2, I raised the question, How can we effectively address the learning needs of today's children in the traditional classroom structure? I also asked a second question: How can we teach the *how* of skills and competencies identified in the SCANS Report? In answering both these questions, I proposed learning stations as a logical solution. Chapter 3 illustrated how you could transform your classroom structure and instructional delivery method, using math stations.

In Section I of this chapter, the goal and structure of multisubject stations is presented. Section II describes the basic multisubject stations' content and physical design. Section III details some multisubject learning station plans that illustrate different ways to use learning stations. The chapter then concludes with some techniques for maximizing the effectiveness of station operations.

The information in this chapter will help you structure a learning environment in which form follows function: skills and competencies are learned *within* and *through* the learning stations structure. The key to successful use of learning stations is the *knowledgeable* and *innovative* use of both technology and volunteers. This allows you and your students to maximize your new roles. For you, this means being free to be a more effective teacher—to coach and have time for substantive conversation with students. For students, it means being involved as active learners.

## SECTION I: GOAL AND STRUCTURE

The goal of multisubject learning stations is to involve children in innovative, relevant, real-world learning, so they will be equipped to function as happy and productive citizens. Students develop *learning how-to-learn skills:* They become self-reliant learners.

In my classroom, I use four to six multisubject learning stations as the primary learning structure for language arts, history, science, and geography with an integrated reading and writing emphasis throughout these content areas. Most often, I design the learning-station plan to blend the subjects into a seamless, multisubject learning process, as opposed to a fragmented one.

Learning stations provide a means for students to accomplish both content learning outcomes (basic skills), while also achieving "workplace know-how" competencies and skills, such as using different types of resources, information, technology, and interpersonal skills.

In order to use stations successfully, students need to use and incorporate the personal qualities of individual responsibility, self-management, sociability, and integrity. When all of these elements are working together, they have the potential to create a powerful learning synergy. This is the power of the learning station concept.

Let's review the key characteristics of learning stations. They use small-group learning, integrated technology applications, volunteers as essential learning resources, and teacher-to-student conversations. The students work at multisubject stations two or three days each week. The station groups are determined on the basis of students' specific interests, topics, table group, or student choice. (See Chapter 2 for a discussion of grouping.) For two or three hours a day, students rotate from station to station, spending approximately 30 to 50 minutes at each one.

## SECTION II: THE SIX MULTISUBJECT LEARNING STATIONS

The stations are so named because of the key learning tool used or primary function. This provides an organizational framework. Keep in mind that it is the *learning content* of each station that *changes* with each new learning-station plan. The basic station framework stays the same to give students necessary stability and predictability. Basic learning-station framework can be used for all curricular levels. The SCANS skills and competencies are integrated throughout the six multisubject stations.

Following is a detailed description of each station, with explanations about goals, equipment, supplies, and other necessary components that you will need when designing a multisubject learning-station plan.

### STATION 1: "BROADCAST NEWS"

#### Station Description and Goal

The "broadcast news" station's goal is to have students develop competencies in communication skills while learning different subjects. Special emphasis is given to students' developing presentation skills, collaborative skills, reporting skills, and self-confidence. To accomplish this, students produce a three-minute videotape report. See Figure 4.1.

#### Station Equipment and Resource Materials

The camcorder, a videotape, 5W's form (an organizational and planning tool that students use as a guide to prepare their report for the "broadcast news" videotape), newspapers, and pull-down maps are the basic materials and equipment. Figure 4.2 illustrates the 5W's form.

**FIGURE 4.1   Station 1: Broadcast News**

**FIGURE 4.2   5W's Reporting Form**

**The 5W's**

News stories are written in an inverted pyramid style. The most important facts of the story are presented in the first or "lead" paragraph. The lead usually answers the questions Who? What? When? Where? and Why? or How? The details of the story flow in a descending order of importance.

Put your news story here.

Who? _____

_____

What? _____

_____

When? _____

_____

Where? _____

_____

Why or How? _____

_____

_____

Reminder: Place this sheet in the quality finished product envelope.

### Station Happenings

When I first used the "broadcast news" station, I would have the students return the production videotapes to my desk. A student suggested that we store videotapes on a shelf at the "broadcast news" station and organize them by topic and date. Having the videotapes lined up like books on a shelf makes them easy to use and saves the teacher and students time. This is an excellent example to illustrate students and myself working together to improve a procedure.

### Student Examples

Imagination thrives at this station. For example, students videotaped an outdoor winter scene to capture an authentic setting for their model of the St. Paul Winter Carnival Ice Palace to use in their Winter Carnival videotape production. Students sometimes bring in their own props and costumes for these productions.

### Assessment and Accountability

The finished three-minute videotape serves as both an assessment and learning accountability tool.

## STATION 2: "HOW'S IT GOING?"

### Station Description and Goals

Station 2 is the basic teaching and small-group discussion station for all core curricula. Its purpose and benefits are much like the book-learning station described in Chapter 3. This station along with the other stations, contributes to achieving the goal of developing skills and competencies in basic skills, thinking skills, and personal qualities. Specifically, this station's goals are to help students develop building knowledge skills through various types of media (learning resources) and to develop greater in-depth learning in all content areas through both teacher-led instruction and teacher-student conversations.

### Station Equipment and Resource Materials

Often I locate this station at the table in the center of the room. This gives me greater visibility and access to most other stations. The materials I routinely use are social studies, science, or English texts, or related resource materials, including magazines, such as *Cobblestone* (a children's history magazine), or Lego materials. The equipment I occasionally use at this station is a VCR, a computer, or a filmstrip viewer.

### Student Materials

Students come to this station with a subject notebook for taking notes, and any necessary assignments that will be used at this station.

### Station Happenings

One of the primary activities at this station is teacher-student discussion. Students learn how to critically discuss by engaging in such discussions. See Figure 4.3 for more information on generating discussion. Although

## FIGURE 4.3   Learning through Discussion

How does discussion help students learn about a story?

This is a question JGB [Junior Great Books] leaders will want to consider carefully. David Bridges, in his book *Education, Democracy, and Discussion,* explains that researchers have found five ways in which discussion builds understanding of a topic.

1. *Pooling information.* All participants—even the best prepared—bring to discussion only partial knowledge of the subject. In discussion, each can pick up information from the others. In Shared Inquiry Discussion and the Curriculum's new interpretive activities, you will frequently observe that when you ask for evidence, one student will bring up a detail in the story that others have forgotten or even misread. All participants gain greater knowledge of the text when you ask one to explain the evidence for an opinion.

2. *Sharing different perspectives.* Participants in discussion have different personal experiences that lead them to different conclusions about a topic. In Shared Inquiry Discussion, these unique experiences lead to a variety of interpretations of a test. The object of discussion, notes Bridges, is "to draw out and to explore as fully as possible this range of perspectives."[1] Bridges observes that ideally the goal is "neither to decide which one is the 'right' view nor to try somehow to synthesize them into a single coherent perspective, but rather to *understand* them in their diversity."[2] In JGB, you can develop understanding of different perspectives by encouraging students to explain their opinions fully and to listen and respond to each other.

3. *Creating new conjectures.* Group discussion involves more than exchanging the ideas we had beforehand. Once we are engaged, once the juices start flowing, new ideas emerge. Discussion can promote learning "by stimulating one's own imagination so that one begins to develop fresh thoughts and ideas for oneself," writes Bridges.[3] The discussion leader's open-mindedness and welcoming attitude toward new ideas helps further this process.

4. *Refutation.* Participants in a discussion not only originate ideas, they also argue about them. The "free interplay of opinion and criticism in discussion" has long been seen as "a necessary condition for the proper testing or the 'purification' of belief," states Bridges.[4] In Shared Inquiry Discussion, because the leader does not act as an authority who designates right and wrong answers, the participants are asked to test ideas and weigh interpretations themselves. This goes beyond pooling information and becoming aware of different perspectives. It involves considering how well supported and how comprehensive each idea is. Does this passage support that idea? Or should it be read differently to support this idea? Does that interpretation illuminate all parts of the story, or only some? You will promote the weighing of ideas when you carefully explore disagreement and invite participants to question and respond to each other directly. Also, your open-minded curiosity serves as a model for how they can approach others' ideas.

Bridges notes that the use of discussion to achieve critical thinking is relatively rare in the classroom, and urges that teachers realize how much "progress in understanding depends on our readiness to expose ourselves to correction."[5] Developing critical thinking through intensive practice is far more important to students than learning "good," standard interpretations of the stories they read.

**FIGURE 4.3  *continued***

5. *The mutual adjustment of opinions.* Finally, participants in discussion react to each other by modifying their thinking. In the light of new information, perspectives, conjectures, and refutations of ideas, fuller understandings of the topic emerge. Bridges warns that "an overbearing, over-dominant chairman" prevents the mutual adjustment of ideas, leaving the group "with an opinion which is in effect the product of a single mind," unimproved by "the collective wisdom of the group" and "the subjective imagination of individual members."[6] The rules of Shared Inquiry Discussion help you avoid shortchanging your group in this way. By following these rules and understanding the learning possibilities they afford, you can make discussion a valuable school experience.

**The Rules of Shared Inquiry Discussion**

1. Only people who have read the story may take part in Shared Inquiry Discussion.
2. Discuss only the story everyone has read.
3. Do not use other people's opinions about the story unless you can back them up with evidence of your own.
4. Leaders may only ask questions; they may not answer them.

Notes:

[1]David Bridges, *Education, Democracy, and Discussion* (Windsor, U.K.: NFER Publishing Company Ltd., 1979), pp. 37–38.
[2]Ibid., p. 38.
[3]Ibid., p. 42.
[4]Ibid., p. 43.
[5]Ibid., p. 44.
[6]Ibid., p. 46.

*Source:* Article copyright 1992 by The Great Books Foundation, a nonprofit educational corporation. The shared inquiry discussion method was developed by the Great Books Foundation to be used in conjunction with the literature published in the Junior Great Books Program and the Great Books Program for adults. For information on these programs and the Great Books Foundation training for discussion leaders, call 1-800-222-5870. Reprinted with permission.

this is designed as a Junior Great Books discussion guide, I have found using parts of this useful for any discussion.

During the first year of implementing learning stations, one of the discussion topics at this station was titled, "Industrial Revolution: Its Effects Today in Education." A comment made by one of my students that kept me going during this time was, "Wow, how can the time pass so fast? I really like this; can we do it again? I really understand what the Industrial Revolution was about and I see its effects on us today." I have found that using the station format to conduct a parent education meeting is an effective way to show parents how learning stations work.

With this station, I can sometimes design the station activities to allow time for me to work with students at other stations. Occasionally, I spend five to seven minutes away from the "How's it going?" station to correct students' work at another station or to complete one-minute observations on students particular working/learning skills at another station. For example, I use a checklist to assess students' technological skills, such as their competency using the cut, copy, and paste functions when working with a computer word-processing program.

### Special Benefits

At this station, the teacher is a necessary and primary resource; there is no substitute. I am at this station 90 percent of the time doing many traditional tasks such as providing instruction, facilitating discussion, checking that work is in, discussing individual problems and successes, and assessing progress. See Figure 4.4.

The small-group setting maximizes the effectiveness of the teacher as coach, guide, and diagnostician, and automatically increases the students' spontaneity, accountability, and conversation. I spend time at this station ensuring that students know why they are doing the work—why it is important—and that they know the process for producing quality work. For example, learning the process for reporting from a news article does not happen simply by reading, nor does it occur by copying sentences from the article. An important step in learning the reporting process is for students to develop the skill of distilling the article's highlights. Also, it is important for students to realize how this distillation skill serves as a building block for effective research.

As students' sense of community develops, they work to help each other succeed. They know who needs reminding, who needs encourage-

**FIGURE 4.4 Station 2: How's It Going?**

ment, and so on. The power of this positive peer influence helps students to take responsibility and pride in their own learning. In addition, there is a collegial work bond established here that cannot be achieved in just whole-group instruction. Student confidence flourishes in this environment because it is almost impossible *not* to "catch them doing something good."

### Student Examples

A couple weeks into learning stations, the students came to the "How's it going?" station with a completed assignment. Jesse, a first-year student in our classroom, had his notebook open to show me his work. He had the work completed but had not followed the instructions. He had incorrect information (the Native-American tribes and clans were not listed separately), he had not used the format that the class agreed on, and he had not met the quality product criteria.

After a brief discussion about those items, I asked him to choose one major tribe to put in order and then rewrite his notebook. A few minutes later, he asked me to look at his work. It was neatly and accurately done and I asked him what he thought. When he said that he knew he had done a good job, I agreed.

His next comment was, "How many do you want me to do this time?" My response was, "Do you see any others that need redoing?" He pointed out another group and he went to work. The second time he showed me his work, he said, "You know, I can do all the groups over."

The attitude change was the most important learning that happened for him that day. At a time like this, the exhilaration and joy I feel renews all the reasons I went into teaching. The one-on-one time with this child to produce this important result was probably three to four minutes at the most.

In this situation, I was operating on a few premises: This is a bright but disinterested student. I needed to keep his job of producing a quality product in small manageable tasks. Some nice things are happening here. The student and I are talking and correcting the problem together. I have made no checks or marks on his work. I believe this setting provides for a more quiet, private, and humane way of working with children, and, finally, there has been no humiliation.

This station also provides opportunities to recognize individual personality traits that make the students the unique persons they are and to exchange a little humor. For example, in Patty's second year in the program, her handwriting improved a great deal. After praising her for her great improvement, I joked with her about how I bet she had spent the whole summer working on that handwriting. She was amused but also proud.

### Assessment and Accountability

Students' completed assignments are used as only one part of assessing their progress and accountability. Another part of assessment accountability is based on my own observation and evaluation of each student's participation in activities at this station. Other tools are station activity videotapes and whole-group or small-group station reports.

## STATION 3: COMPUTER

### Station Description and Goals

Specifically, this station, with the computer as the primary learning tool, helps students develop skills in content areas using all three learning modes: building knowledge, practicing skills, and putting it all together. The technology helps students pace their own learning and increase their learning productivity. For example, students experience the ease of writing and rewriting using a word-processing program. This gives them a reflective and creative method to produce a final quality product.

### Station Equipment and Resource Materials

The number and type of computers can vary depending on what you have available. I use as basic equipment a mini-lab of two computers networked to one printer and the computer at my desk as an auxiliary computer station. Basic software includes word-processing, database, spreadsheet programs, problem-solving, skill development, and simulation programs. A printer, paper, and individual student disks are necessary at this station. See Figures 4.5 and 4.6.

### Student Materials

Students come to this station prepared with information for word processing, database entries, or graphics work.

### Station Happenings

Students arrive prepared to work. This station is one of the best examples of on-task, self-directed learning within a very collegial and relaxed learning environment.

### Assessment and Accountability

Printed copies of work produced at this station are usually put into the quality finished product envelope for written performance assessment. Other assessments, which frequently serve as a means of accountability, are oral performances, work stored on the students' personal computer disk, and anecdotal comments and observation checklists completed by

**FIGURE 4.5    Station 3: Computer**

me. Some software has a management system that keeps track of student progress. Individual student progress can be viewed on the screen or hard copy.

## STATION 4: MULTIMEDIA

### *Station Description and Goals*

In either an individual or a collaborative effort, students work with a variety of technologies that provide opportunities for using the three different learning modes. This station's purpose is to expand and enhance students' learning and basic skills while using a variety of media.

**FIGURE 4.6   Station 3: Auxiliary Computer**

Teachers can adapt the various learning tools and resources to help students in achieving a specific learning task at this station. Students benefit from experiencing the versatility and innovation these tools provide, and they often strategize even more uses as they begin to construct their own learning experience.

### Station Equipment and Resource Materials

The multimedia station uses a variety of media equipment, including audiotape player/recorder, videocassette player, two computers, camcorder, filmstrip viewer/projector, laser disk player, audiotapes, videotapes, filmstrips, CD-ROM discs, and videodiscs. See Figure 4.7.

### Student Materials

Each student usually brings a notebook and pencil to this station. If students need additional materials, this information is included on their learning station plan.

**FIGURE 4.7    Station 4: Multimedia**

Other Station Equipment

| Monitor |
| Laser Disk |
| VCR |

| Computer |
| CD-ROM |
| Filmstrip |

### Station Happenings

Jeremy was researching Patrick Henry for an assignment. He needed more detailed information. Jeremy shared with me, quite proud of his discovery, information he tapped into using Colonial Times computer databases. He had decided to examine the "Patriot" file and asked if he could use the "Find" command to get further information. This is another example of a student directing and thinking about his own learning. When he was examining the files on the Colonial Times database, Jeremy made the connection that there were files that could serve as a resource for his getting more detailed information about Patrick Henry.

### Student Examples

Students become very comfortable using a variety of media equipment as learning resources for doing research and gathering more information.

### Assessment and Accountability

Some assessment and accountability products used at this station are student notes from a videotape or filmstrip, quizzes, and completed workbook lessons that accompany laser discs.

## STATION 5: EXPERIENTIAL

### Station Description and Goals

One goal of this station is to provide hands-on opportunities to enhance students' understanding of science concepts and cultures in the world. This station helps students develop interpersonal skills as they work together sharing resources. In addition, students apply creative thinking and problem-solving techniques to implement a variety of action plans.

### Station Equipment and Resource Materials

Equipment at this station varies depending on the hands-on task. For example, a cooking station requires all of the utensils and ingredients for the recipe, whereas a science experiment might call for planting seeds, potting plants, or Lego construction pieces. See Figure 4.8.

### Station Happenings

We use this station for hands-on, experiential learning and tangible assessment activities. Also, the types of activities at this station many times help to build a sense of community in the classroom. Specific uses include Lego building, science experiments, map drawing, horticulture experiments, sewing, and historical and ethnic cooking. I often use parent volunteers at this station.

### Student Examples

A student with a learning disability explained mechanical advantage to students in his group. He went on to tell how to build for either power or speed in a Lego Logo gear experiment. Another time, four girls at a station built change of motion gear models and then, on their own initiative, improved on the experiment by motorizing them.

### Assessment and Accountability

Students will usually have a finished product such as prepared food, experiment results, a painting, a map, a Lego project, and so on.

**FIGURE 4.8    Station 5: Experiential**

## STATION 6: MULTIPURPOSE

### *Station Description and Goals*

The primary goal is to accommodate students' individual learning styles and needs. Another goal is to provide students opportunities to practice individual responsibility and self-management skills. This station is designed to give students time to finish tasks either from other stations or whole-group learning.

### *Station Equipment and Resource Materials*

Equipment and resources vary according to the specific learning task at this station. I often use a volunteer at this station.

### *Station Happenings*

When we need a choice station, which is designed to give students independent work time, I most often locate it at the multipurpose station. A choice station example may include students working on projects, doing research with an electronic database, making a title page for their project, or completing a whole-group instruction activity such as practicing their spelling.

Station 6 stays rather flexible to serve many different purposes, all determined by the students needs. See Figure 4.9.

### *Student Examples*

Another purpose of the multipurpose station is to provide an opportunity for doing tasks that require greater amounts of time to complete or adult supervision. For example, at the experiential station when students are sewing pillows, I include the multipurpose station as a sewing station so I can have two sewing stations.

**FIGURE 4.9    Station 6: Multipurpose ("Homey" area, shown here, is frequently part of this station.)**

### Assessment and Accountability

Depending on the task, there may not always be an immediate product. What students produce will depend on the station activity. For example, it may be correcting misspelled words and punctuation on a descriptive paragraph, and the product might consist of a hard copy of both the original and corrected paragraph.

# SECTION III: MULTISUBJECT STATION PLANS

Below are some samples of multisubject learning-station plans. These plans include students' group instructions that describe the station content. I have included additional information in these sample plans for the reader of this book. It includes the station's learning mode, goal, equipment, supplies, and happenings.

The learning-station plans could be used at any time of the year. These plans are written for an elementary intermediate level but, with minor adjustments, they are relevant for grades 2 through 8. The learning stations are the organizational framework where the content of the station can be adapted to a specific ability or grade level.

These station plans show the three most common ways the multisubject stations can be used:

1. Interdisciplinary learning stations
2. Single discipline learning stations
3. Single learning mode learning stations

A learning-station plan requires approximately three and one-half hours in order for each station group to rotate through all six stations. However, you have the option of using the stations any way you like. For example, three station movements a day (each group completing three stations), or using only one station a day or all six in a day. As you read through the plans, you will see the integral relationship between *students' effective use of communication skills and the stations' successful operation.*

# SECTION IIIA: INTERDISCIPLINARY LEARNING STATIONS

### Sample Station Plan: Discrimination

The following example uses *Anne Frank in the World: I Can Make a Difference* as a medium for investigating discrimination themes. It can be taught with or without Hypercard. (Please refer to Chapter 6 for Hypercard details.) Notice how a theme or broad topic can be an organizing mechanism to use with interdisciplinary learning stations.

*Station 1: "Broadcast News"*
Discrimination in Our Everyday Lives

### Learning Modes
Putting It All Together, Practicing Skills

### Student Group Instructions
Share with each other your example and any plans and props you have brought along about the topic "Discrimination and Racism in Our World Today."

Remember, we decided that we wanted a longer time period for the "broadcast news" videotape titled "Discrimination in Our Everyday Lives." In your actual broadcast, remember your introduction to your audience. Introduce your topic and group members. You may want to use a map to show the location of your story. Be very careful with the camcorder and use your best cooperative skills with other group members.

### Station Goals
This station's specific goals are for students to identify examples of discrimination or racism in today's society and to produce a videotape reporting on discrimination example.

### SCANS Goals
Workplace competencies of selecting resources for goal-relevant activities, interpersonal skills of participating as a member of a team, acquiring and using information, and basic skills of reading, listening, and speaking

### Station Equipment and Resources
Daily newspapers, camcorder, videotape, and maps

### Student Materials
Paper and pencils, and 5W's form

### Station Happenings
Each student comes to this station with an article from a magazine or newspaper. For the past three weeks, as one of their assignments from their weekly homework packet, the students have submitted a newspaper or magazine article that identifies discrimination.

Students are using their knowledge of discrimination and racism to identify real-world examples. At this station, they find an example of significance to them and communicate the message of the story using their own words, pictures, or a short skit. They will also identify the geographic location of the story. How to report on an article without just copying sentences is a skill that I teach at the "How's it going?" station.

### Assessment and Accountability
The finished videotape

### Station 2: "How's It Going?"
Literature Discussion

### Learning Mode
Putting It All Together

### Student Group Instructions
We will discuss your group's assigned reading from your literature selection. Bring your book and your reading journals.

### Station Goals
Students will expand their knowledge base about World War II from a perspective other than a history text format.

### SCANS Goals
Basic skills of reading and speaking

### Station Equipment and Resources
The teacher is to lead or facilitate the discussion. Include any artifacts or interesting facts about these books, such as more background about the authors.

### Student Materials
*Number the Stars, Journey to America, Devil's Arithmetic, The Upstairs Room,* and students' reading journals

### Station Happenings
Students will report where they are in their discussion books and discuss the assigned reading. I always encourage them to write down any happenings or words that they might not understand, along with the page number, so that we can easily refer to the exact part of the book. This is a practice students develop from their participation in Junior Great Books.

Other items students may include in their journals are key events in the book, their own feelings, insights and any information (such as interesting places or vocabulary they came upon in their reading) and sketches or illustrations of favorite parts.

In these small-group book discussions, it is a time for sharing ideas and information with each other in an atmosphere of comfort, enjoyment, and respect of others ideas. Being able to do this is evidence of the students' appropriate preparation for the discussion. I hope that each person, myself included, will end up with new knowledge, insights, and ideas about the book as well as his or her world on a broader scale.

### Assessment and Accountability
Student contributions to group discussion and entries in their reading journals

### Station 3: Computer
I Can Make a Difference (With Hypercard)

### Learning Mode
Building Knowledge

### Student Group Instructions
Explore the Hypercard stack entitled *Anne Frank in the World: I Can Make A Difference* using the buttons to move between screens and to view video clips. You may want to share the controls by taking turns at the keyboard.

Take the time to discuss each card with your group. Do you understand the vocabulary? What does *discrimination* really mean to you? The final cards in the Hypercard stack ask you to write your own thoughts on discrimination.

Each member of the group should enter his or her own thoughts using complete sentences on the same card (one card is provided for each station group). Please print out your group's card and put it in the quality finished product envelope.

### Station Goals
Students will navigate through the *Anne Frank in the World: I Can Make a Difference* Hypercard stack. They will be exposed to the four themes of discrimination (listed at Station 6 on page 92) and answer questions in an interactive experience using the teacher prepared Hypercard stack.

### SCANS Goals
Basic reading and speaking, and thinking skills of reasoning

### Station Equipment and Resources
Computers with Hypercard and QuickTime software, *Anne Frank in the World: I Can Make A Difference* (Hypercard stack, teacher prepared)

### Student Materials
None

### Station Happenings
Students will navigate through the Hypercard stack and discuss the four themes of discrimination.

### Assessment and Accountability
A hard copy of students answers entered on Hypercard placed in the quality finished product envelope

### Station 3: Computer
Discrimination Themes (Without Hypercard)

### Learning Mode
Building Knowledge

### Student Group Instructions

Choose a group member to read Eve Bunting's *Terrible Things* aloud to the group. After reading the story, share experiences that you may have had when you felt discrimination or when you may have intervened to prevent discrimination.

Each group member should choose one of the Four Discrimination Themes Activity Sheets and write a short narrative, draw a picture, or make a collage from the magazine or newspaper articles at the station to illustrate your discrimination theme.

### Station Goals

Students will know and use the vocabulary of the four discrimination themes. They will individually interpret one of the themes in writing or visually.

### SCANS Goals

Basic skills of reading and listening, and thinking skills of reasoning

### Station Equipment and Resources

*Terrible Things* by Eve Bunting, Four Themes of Discrimination activity sheets, old magazines, newspapers, scissors, and glue

### Student Materials

Pencils or markers

### Station Happenings

Students will relate the four themes of discrimination, first to a children's story and then to their own knowledge of the world around them. The four themes are each distinct and yet related, and help students make connections to discrimination in the world today. The students extend their knowledge of discrimination themes by interpreting these themes in a personal way on an activity sheet.

### Assessment and Accountability

A completed Four Themes of Discrimination activity sheet

### Station 4: Multimedia
Symbols, Shapes, and Signs

### Learning Mode
Building Knowledge

### Student Group Instructions

Use the symbols poster to familiarize your group with a variety of the symbols or logos that we see in the world around us. Think about the way the Jewish people were forced to wear the yellow star during Anne Frank's lifetime. Was this a positive or negative use of the star as a symbol?

Using a graphics program on the computer, design a symbol for yourself, your family, or your station group and print your finished design. Make sure the symbol is meaningful to you and others, and be ready to explain your choice at the end of stations today. Save your symbols on your disks and put the printed copy in the quality finished product envelope.

### Station Goals
Students will understand that symbols can be used for positive and negative purposes. They will also realize that symbols can play a part in discrimination both in the past and today. They will create a collection of symbols that have meaning to them using a Draw program on the computer.

### SCANS Goals
Thinking skills of creativity and reasoning

### Station Equipment and Resources
Two computers (used in pairs), drawing program such as Microsoft Works Draw or Claris Works Draw, printer, and symbol sheets (If you do not have computers available, students may use paper to draw their symbol or logo.)

### Student Materials
None

### Station Happenings
Students will apply their knowledge of symbols and their uses to design their own personal or group symbol. They will use a computer drawing program with which they are familiar to illustrate and print out their symbol to share with the rest of their classmates.

### Assessment and Accountability
Printed copies of the symbols designed at this station

### Station 5: Experiential
Design and Build Anne's Annex Models

### Learning Mode
Putting It All Together

### Student Group Instructions
Mrs. Sanchez, John's mother, will be at this station to help you do quality work on selecting a floor plan and building your own three-dimensional model of some part of the Annex.

Decide, as a group, if you want to review and/or write out with Mrs. Sanchez the basic steps for doing this task. This model-making task requires good planning. Do you want to each make one or do you want to work in pairs? You will be working with floor areas by comparing measurements of the scale floor plans of the Annex to your model. Are you working with ratios or proportions? That fraction work was worth it, right?

Use a pencil, paper, and calculator to convert the measurements from the original floor plan to your cardboard rectangle. (Mrs. Sanchez will help you with this.) Remember the carpenter's rule: Measure twice; cut once.

If you do not finish, please store your work on the numbered station shelf that matches your station group number. Please feel free to use the decorating materials on the shelf for building walls and making furniture.

Your final room or floor design will be assessed for accuracy to original scale (ratios) and neatness.

### Station Goals
Students will practice using a calculator to convert floor measurements to scale on a model of the Annex. They will create a replica of some room or group of rooms that were part of Anne Frank's living area during her stay at the Annex.

### SCANS Goals
Basic skills of math, thinking skills of reasoning, creativity, and seeing things in the mind's eye

### Station Equipment and Resources
Calculators, floor plans, rulers, cardboard squares, fabric, wood scraps, assorted materials, glue, tape, toothpicks, tacks, and construction paper

### Student Materials
None

### Station Happenings
Students decide which part of the Annex they would like to create. They will choose a method for assembling the Annex model so that all group members are included in the creation. The parent volunteer can help the students convert the measurements to the new cardboard floor rectangle. They can then measure and mark with a pencil the appropriate wall placements.

Time management and planning will be important at this station in order that a good portion of the model can be built during the station time period.

### Assessment and Accountability
The students and I will check finished products for correct scale and neatness.

### Station 6: Multipurpose
Journal Writing

*Learning Mode*
Practicing Skills

*Student Group Instructions*
Choose one of the four themes of discrimination:

1. Discrimination is cruel and irrational.
2. It is the ordinary citizen who discriminates.
3. Discrimination is a matter of personal choice.
4. Discrimination, prejudice, and racism not only existed in the past but they still exist today.

   With a partner or independently, write at least a page in your journal about your thoughts, beliefs, and feelings on this theme. Please cite examples from your literature reading.

*Station Goals*
Students will have the opportunity to reflect on what the four themes of discrimination mean to them.

*SCANS Goals*
Basic skills of reading and writing, thinking skills of creative thinking and reasoning, personal quality of integrity

*Station Equipment and Resources*
Four Themes of Discrimination sheets

*Student Materials*
Reading journals and pencils

*Station Happenings*
Students can begin this station with a quiet discussion of the meaning of the four discrimination themes. The students can then find a quiet place in the room to write in their journals for the remainder of the station time. (Prior to this, four themes need to be introduced in a whole-group setting by the teacher.)

*Assessment and Accountability*
Entries in reading journals

## SECTION IIIB: SINGLE DISCIPLINE LEARNING STATIONS

The previous six learning stations were built around a single topic—discrimination—with an interdisciplinary approach. All three modes of learning were used, and various disciplines—such as American history, social studies, and science—were included in the activities. In addition, the *how* of the SCANS skills and competencies was built into the learning-station activities.

In this section, the learning stations are organized around a single discipline—world awareness—a combination of history and current events. The following learning-station plans include: (1) station learning mode, (2) student group instructions (station content description), (3) station goals, and (4) SCANS goals. In the interest of brevity, I have omitted the listing of station equipment and resources, student materials, assessment and accountability, and some station happenings. Up to now, these elements have been listed to demonstrate the similarity between a traditional lesson plan and a learning-station plan. At this point, it will be assumed that the reader understands that these elements are intrinsic to all station plans.

### Sample Station Plan: Social Studies

**Station 1: "Broadcast News"**
International Events

**Learning Mode**
Putting It All Together

**Student Group Instructions**
Please select two international news events to report on in your group's news broadcast. If you can find any news about India or surrounding countries for your broadcast, please use these.

Discuss and plan how you will put together your *four-minute* broad-cast. (Note that the broadcast time has been increased from our usual three minutes to four minutes.) Emily suggested we increase the time because of our special guest from India.

Remember to use your 5W's form for each article. Try to write just what you remember from one or two readings of your article. Be *careful* with the camcorder and be *kind* to each other. Prepare well. Make sure you can pronounce all words and know what the words mean before you use them. Practice telling the news in your own words. In your presentation's introduction, identify yourselves and the title of the news article.

**Station Goals**
Students will organize and produce a short videotape on international news. They will present the four-minute broadcast using accurate vo-cabulary and facts.

**SCANS Goals**
Workplace competencies of acquiring and evaluating information, apply-ing technology to specific tasks, basic skills of reading, listening, and speaking, and personal qualities of responsibility and self-management

### Station Happenings

Students need to make quick decisions and share responsibilities at this station in order to finish in the allotted time period. They work collaboratively to choose their news articles and to distribute jobs, such as who is going to be behind or in front of the camera. When the group is ready to tape, they post the "TAPING" sign so the rest of the stations are quiet while they tape their production.

### Station 2: "How's It Going?"
Telecommunications Readiness

### Learning Mode
Building Knowledge

(Prior to coming to the "How's it going?" station, the whole group watched a short introductory *National Geographic Kids Network* videotape. I have also demonstrated the key features of the *Hello!* computer software to the whole group.)

### Student Group Instructions

At this station, we will read your *Hello! Kids Handbook* and discuss specific terms such as telecommunications, electronic mail, and global address. Next, we will read about our first telecommunications activity and take a few minutes using the *Hello!* program to practice finding global addresses for our school, Minneapolis, Duluth, and St. Cloud. Bring your social studies notebook if you want to take notes. This is an example of a time (while students are finding these global addresses) that I can use to check progress at other stations.

### Station Goals

Students will be able to use the map features on the *Hello!* program to find their global address by applying the directional concepts longitude, latitude, degrees, and minutes.

### SCANS Goals

Workplace competencies of using technology and interpersonal skills to process information, gather data, and organize and maintain files; use thinking skills to reason and solve problems and use efficient learning techniques and the personal quality of self-management

### Station Happenings

The *Hello!* program is an excellent resource for expanding children's technology use skills, as well as their map-making, graphing, and research skills. During the year, students use this program's map-making and graphing features for other projects or learning tasks. (Please see Chapter 6 for more details about the *Hello!* program.)

### Station 3: Computer
North America Database

### Learning Mode
Practicing Skills
(Prior to using this station, the whole group views an introductory database videotape followed by a teacher/student discussion.)

### Student Group Instructions
Use what you have learned about both the *program* and *data* disks to work with the North America Databases. For additional help, I encourage you to look at the following posted resource sheets: Regions of North America, Database Overview, and Sample Record.

You may want to take a few minutes to use the Browse command to explore the different records in this file. Remember, as a class, we decided that everyone would complete the getting started activity and then each of you may choose one activity to complete from the following list:

1. Investigating Political History

2. Investigating Ethnic Groups

3. Investigating Economies

4. Investigating Living Standards

Please check your two completed activity sheets for quality work and place them in the quality finished product envelope.

### Station Goals
Students will locate information on North American regions using a computer database.

### SCANS Goals
Workplace competencies of using technology to acquire information, interpreting and working with data, basic skills of reading, thinking skills of decision making and knowing how to learn

### Station 4: Multimedia
World Events

### Learning Mode
Building Knowledge

*NewsCurrents* is a weekly filmstrip that serves as an important component in making connections with everything else we study in world news. See Chapter 7 for complete details about *NewsCurrents*.

### Student Group Instructions

Please check the topics in the *NewsCurrents* guide for this week's filmstrip. Decide which two stories your group will use and who is going to read the script for each frame. As you are learning more about these stories from the filmstrip, think about which story your group would like to report on to the rest of the class. You will need your social studies notebook and a pencil to take notes on the two selected topics. (Remember to title and date these notes in your notebook.)

### Station Goals

Students will gain more information about current news in their world.

### SCANS Goals

Basic skills of reading, listening, writing, and speaking: students use of technology skills, acquire and evaluate data, and practice reasoning and problem solving

### Station 5: Experiential

Speaker from India

### Learning Mode

Building Knowledge

### Student Group Instructions

Today, Karyn Kollins will be visiting with you about a few cultural and political happenings that took place while she was in India. She will also talk to you about common foods, plants, and animals in India. She will describe to you what a typical day at work as a nurse was like. She will have artifacts and pictures to share with you.

### Station Goals

Students will learn about the general culture and the political system of India today. Students will practice questioning skills.

### SCANS Goals

Basic skills of listening and speaking

### Station Happenings

Before stations begin, I remind students about what is expected when a visitor comes to the classroom. They are to practice proper listening and questioning skills during the speaker's presentation. I ask them to follow her directions about touching or not touching the artifacts. The first couple of times before we have a speaker, we discuss general appropriate and inappropriate questions. Sometimes I have them jot down a few questions beforehand. (See Figure 4.3.) Something else that happens here is that students see how important it is to be able to communicate clearly and ask the right questions.

*Station 6: Multipurpose*
Beads from Around the World

*Learning Mode*
Building Knowledge and Practicing Skills

*Student Group Instructions*
At this station, we will look at beads from India and surrounding countries and learn more about their uses, how they are made, and their
origins. Also, each group may make Sharbat, a traditional Indian iced fruit
drink.

*Station Goals*
Students will learn more about India's culture.

*SCANS Goals*
Thinking skills of seeing things in the mind's eye and knowing how to
learn, and personal quality of responsibility

*Station Happenings*
This is a station where the motivation, interest, and opportunity for in-
depth learning happens. Also, students start to think along the lines of
how valuable a variety of people are to every part of the learning process.

## SECTION IIIC: SINGLE LEARNING MODE LEARNING STATIONS

Each of the learning-station plans in this section focuses on *one* of the
three learning modes: building knowledge, practicing skills, or putting it
all together. For example, in the first station plan, each station is designed
to integrate the building knowledge mode throughout all subjects. In the
second learning-station plan, the single learning mode of practicing skills
is integrated throughout each station.

### Sample Station Plan: Building Knowledge

*Station 1: "Broadcast News"*
President's Cabinet

*Learning Mode*
Building Knowledge

*Student Group Instructions*
Please title your notebook page "President's Cabinet" and then find Frame
3 on this week's *NewsCurrents* filmstrip. Record the names and titles of
people in the president's cabinet in your notebook. Review your work
and then go on to answer these questions. How many cabinet members
are there? Name our two political parties. Is there anything else that any

of you want to record in your notebook? When questions are completed, place your notebook on my desk. Thank you.

### Station Goals
Students will learn about the structure of the executive branch of the U.S. government. They will become familiar with some of the cabinet members that have recently taken office.

### SCANS Goals
Basic skills of reading, listening, writing

### Station 2: "How's It Going?"
Effective Editorials

### Learning Mode
Building Knowledge

### Student Group Instructions
Today we'll continue learning about guidelines for producing an effective editorial. Next, we will use these guidelines to examine a few editorials from the newspaper. Please bring your English notebook for taking notes.

### Station Goals
Students will increase their understanding of what an editorial is and learn basic techniques for producing effective editorials. Students will review the concepts of point of view and the difference between fact and opinion statements.

### SCANS Goals
Workplace competencies of interpreting and evaluating information, basic skills of listening and speaking, thinking skills of creative thinking and reasoning

### Station 3: Computer
Where in the USA Is Carmen San Diego?

### Learning Mode
Building Knowledge

### Student Group Instructions
When you use *Where in the USA Is Carmen San Diego?* please work with a partner. Remember to write down clues and new facts. Finally, save your game before you leave the station.

### Station Goals
This software expands students' general knowledge about the United States.

### SCANS Goals
Basic skills of reading, thinking skills of problem solving, and personal qualities of demonstrating politeness and understanding in a group setting

### Station Happenings
Students enjoy problem solving with different crime scenarios while building knowledge about different time periods and areas of the United States. They must use the reference books provided with the game to gain information in solving the crimes. They are required to write down new information (a minimum of two facts) in their social studies notebooks. This practice helps students develop information-gathering habits. About once a month, for assessment purposes, students present these facts at either the "How's it going?" station or the "broadcast news" station.

*Where in the USA Is Carmen San Diego?* is a very motivating and exciting learning resource for students and is often used during choice time. (Choice time is explained in more detail in Chapter 7.)

### Station 4: Multimedia
Science and Structures

### Learning Mode
Building Knowledge

### Student Group Instructions
Today you will view the *3-2-1 Contact* videotape on building structures. Watch carefully how to build a structure for strength, flexibility, or stability. Also, see if there is discussion about such terms as *center of gravity* and *friction*. Take notes if you want.

When you have finished viewing the tape, use the computer on my desk to key in your station number, your names, and two to three interesting facts about the video.

For proofreading, remember one person is to read the group's entries while the rest of you listen. Revise. Then, list what each person did. For example, if Jason read your group's entries to the group, the word *proofreader* should appear after his name. Place a hard copy in the quality finished product envelope. Please clean up the desktop for the next group. Only the File name "Structures" should appear at the top of the screen.

(If no computer is available, students could write out this information.)

### Station Goals
Students will gain knowledge on proper building criteria: strength, flexibility, and stability.

### SCANS Goals
Basic skills of listening, writing, and speaking, thinking skills of decision making and knowing how to learn, personal quality of responsibility

*Station 5: Experiential*
Where in the World?

*Learning Mode*
Building Knowledge

*Student Group Instructions*
Enjoy playing the Where in the World? game. Select the countries and language game to play with. Remember to use good sportsmanship and help partners only if they ask.

*Station Goals*
Students will learn country names, locations, and languages in a game format.

*SCANS Goals*
Basic skills of reading, listening, and speaking, thinking skills of decision making and knowing how to learn, and personal quality of sociability.

*Station Happenings*
During choice time, students enjoy playing this game. There are six games and each of these contains several levels of difficulty. These games focus on world awareness such as countries, their capitals, major imports and exports, languages, and religions.

*Station 6: Multipurpose*
*Cobblestone* Reading

*Learning Mode*
Building Knowledge

*Student Group Instructions*
Today at this station you will have an opportunity to use the *Cobblestone Index*. (Note to readers: *Cobblestone* is a children's history magazine.) Check for any articles relating to the Industrial Age.

What are some words, topics, or people you might use as key descriptors to find this information? How does this relate to using an electronic database such as the "Discussion Book Database"? What are other resources you might use to help you with descriptors?

Review articles with a friend, or by yourself, and jot down any notes of interest, plus the month and year of the *Cobblestone* issue and the title of the article and page numbers. Thank you.

*Station Goals*
Students will learn to use a magazine index to locate information on specific topics. *Cobblestone* has a CD-ROM disk that contains 14 years of *Cobblestone* issues. Included on this disk is a search menu so students can do a topic search and access the text.

### SCANS Goals

Basic competencies of using materials efficiently to acquire information, basic skills of reading and writing, and thinking skills of knowing how to learn

### Station Happenings

Students will brainstorm about words that could be used to locate information about the Industrial Age. They may think of names of people associated with the Industrial Age, inventions, dates, and locations of important events, or just scan the pages of the index to see what interests them.

This work really activates any prior knowledge and sometimes sends students looking for information in their social studies textbook to relate to the index topics. They will then locate the article in the proper issue of *Cobblestone* and read it individually or in pairs. Good notetaking is emphasized and rewarded at this station.

## Sample Station Plan: Practicing Skills

### Station 1: "Broadcast News"

Literature Presentation, Technology and Assessment Skills (Producing Videotape Presentations)

### Learning Mode

Practicing Skills

### Student Group Instructions

At this station I would like you to view the book conference videotape of *My Brother Sam.* Next, discuss and critique this presentation using the standard presentation criteria. From your experience in producing videotape presentations, discuss what you would change and how you could make this videotape better. Don't forget the capabilities of the camcorder.

Each group will have an opportunity to do a "retake" of this videotape, so plan carefully. Please put your group's "retake" plans in the quality finished product envelope.

### Station Goals

Students will practice discussion and assessment skills.

### SCANS Goals

Interpersonal skill of teamwork, understanding of technological systems, thinking skills for decision making and problem solving, and personal qualities of responsibility and self-management

### Station 2: "How's It Going?"

Industrial Revolution

*Learning Mode*
Practicing Skills

*Student Group Instructions*
At this station, we will be discussing the chapters titled "New Inventions and Industries" and "A Growing Population" in our social studies text. Please bring your notes from this morning's whole-group instruction concerning these chapters. Let's think about the Industrial Revolution and its influence and effects on us today.

*Station Goals*
Students will extend their knowledge of the Industrial Revolution from earlier readings and discussions to theorize short-term and long-term effects.

*SCANS Goals*
Basic skills of listening and speaking, thinking skills of creative thinking and reasoning

*Station 3: Computer*
Historical Machine Research

*Learning Mode*
Practicing Skills

*Student Group Instructions*
You may choose to word-process your historical machine research paper or to draw your machine. If you need more time for research, this might be a good time to do it. Please use the books from the research table: *Inventions* (Steven Caney), *National Geographic Index,* or *The Way Things Work* (David Macaulay). You may also use *Grolier's Electronic Encyclopedia.* Please remember our research guidelines.

*Station Goals*
Students will produce a written report or graphic representation of an invention.

*SCANS Goals*
Workplace competencies of applying technology to task, organizing and communicating information, basic skills of reading and writing, thinking skills of decision making, and personal qualities of self-management

*Station 4: Multimedia*
Choice

*Learning Mode*
Practicing Skills

### Student Group Instructions

At this station, if you have not read up to the agreed-upon page, you may wish to use this time for reading in the book, *Lyddie*, by Katherine Patterson. Since everyone is reading this book, it is everyone's responsibility to keep up with our agreed-upon page reading deadlines. If you are keeping up, please feel free to work on any other tasks you may have. (See Chapter 5 for choice station details.)

### Station Goals

Students will select a learning activity that they need to do.

### SCANS Goals

Workplace competencies of time allocation, thinking skills of decision making and knowing how to learn, and personal qualities of responsibility and self-management

### Station 5: Experiential

Building Structures

### Learning Mode

Practicing Skills

### Student Group Instructions

At this station, examine how to build different structures using Legos. Experiment by building the different structures shown in the Structures sheets on your table to find what makes a sturdy structure. For more information, use the *Lego Resource* book if you would like. Another resource is the *"3-2-1 Contact"* videotape on structures.

### Station Goals

Students will understand concepts for building sturdy structures.

### SCANS Goals

Workplace competencies of identifying and planning resources, basic skills of reading and speaking, thinking skills of problem solving and reasoning, and personal qualities of responsibility and self-esteem

### Station 6: Multipurpose

Concentration

### Learning Mode

Practicing Skills

### Student Group Instructions

At this station, you may play the Concentration game to reinforce some of the vocabulary that you have encountered in historical machines research, learning about structures, and the Industrial Revolution.

*Station Goals*
Students will build familiarity with vocabulary terms.

*SCANS Goals*
Basic skills of reading and speaking, thinking skills of problem solving, and personal qualities of demonstrating friendliness and politeness in group settings

## SECTION IV: IMPLEMENTATION OF MULTISUBJECT LEARNING STATIONS

### Arranging the Room for Multisubject Stations

As we discussed in Chapters 2 and 3, the major criteria for arranging any kind of station are (1) easy access to learning equipment and resources, (2) easy mobility for children and equipment, and (3) a comfortable, small-group interactive learning environment. These criteria are important to serve the learning needs of students and for you to create effective learning spaces. Students can be an excellent resource in helping you achieve effective station arrangements.

### Initial Training Procedures

The ultimate goal in training the students to use learning stations of any kind is to establish good station work habits. To achieve this goal, you may want to refer to the specific training procedures detailed in Chapter 2 under Training the Students. Also, in Chapter 5, laying the groundwork learning-station plans are designed to be used for learning-station training. The focus is on organization and following directions—two skills necessary to use stations successfully.

A general recommendation: At first, keep it simple and move slowly.

### Developing and Revising a Continuous and Workable Learning Plan

Students learn at different rates. Usually, the station period of 30 to 50 minutes is sufficient for all students to complete the learning task. However, if students do not finish a station, the structure allows the flexibility—due to its interchangeable parts and downsizing features—to handle these situations in a variety of ways. Most likely, each teacher will handle these situations differently. Here are some general techniques that I use:

- When a few students need to finish two or three different tasks, I create a choice station so students can complete these tasks.
- When everyone needs to finish a specific station, we repeat the same station in the next learning station plan. This is especially

appropriate if the station involves mostly group work and requires a lot of extra learning resources, materials, and equipment.

- When I know beforehand that I will need to increase the length of work time, I will plan for the same task at two stations, giving the students a total of one hour to work.

- When I need to introduce new software or hardware, I may create an introductory software or hardware learning station at the "How's it going?" station. (See Chapter 2 for other options.)

### Student Preparation Work for Particular Stations

Sometimes students need to do preparation work prior to using a station. I use three different methods to help students prepare: homework packets, whole-group instruction, and a learning station.

### Homework Packet Example

If the preparation requires bringing in a newspaper article to use at the "Broadcast News" station, or yarn for use at the weaving station, I use the weekly homework packet to accomplish this type of preparation. This multidisciplinary packet is sent home with students at the beginning of the week and is due on Friday. (Please see Chapter 7 for further details on homework packets.)

Prior to using Station 1: "Broadcast News"—World Awareness, the students have clipped two newspaper articles about international news and brought them to school in their homework packets.

### Whole-Group Instruction and Learning-Station Examples

In preparation for word processing a business letter at the computer station, students are introduced to the parts of a business letter in a teacher-led whole-group instruction. Next, at the experiential station, students write a rough draft of their business letter. Finally, in a new set of multisubject learning-station plans, students bring their rough draft to word-process at Station 3, Computer.

### What Students Like about Multisubject Learning Stations

- Students like being able to talk and discuss things, especially at the "How's it going?" station.

- Students like the responsibility of being a part of assessing their own work.

- Students like having the teacher listen to them.

- Students like the teacher sharing and being very clear about quality performance learning standards.

- Students like feeling that they are having fun while really learning more.

- Students like being trusted to work independently.
- Students feel honored when I solicit their thoughts and opinions. They realize their thoughts and opinions really count when their ideas are used.
- Students like being recognized for their contributions!

# chapter

# 5

# *Customizing Learning Stations*

As my journey in developing stations progressed, I became more skilled at designing learning stations. I saw the logic in downsizing even more of the whole-group learning activities. For example, my experience had always been to test in the whole-group setting. However, as I refined the station plan idea, I realized that many of these traditional activities could be easily handled and enhanced by doing them at the stations.

In terms of testing, I found that when I downsized the class to groups of seven or eight, I was able to teach testing strategies as the students were taking a test. Therefore, as Chapters 3 and 4 showed how core curricula fit into station learning, this chapter shows how stations can be used for other traditional classroom activities. Over the years, I have developed learning-station plans for the following activities and include them in this chapter:

1. Laying the Groundwork
2. Choice
3. Project
4. Testing and Performance Learning Assessment
5. Presentation Rehearsal
6. Art and Culture

## LAYING THE GROUNDWORK LEARNING STATIONS

Organization is crucial to make stations work effectively. When you first begin the station format, children need to learn the basic elements of self-directed learning. The laying the groundwork stations begin to teach the children how to:

1. Follow instructions
2. Organize
3. Access information (research )
4. Use equipment and learning resources
5. Make presentations
6. Assess learning
7. Work independently

I have included here three laying the groundwork station plan examples. You may wish to develop your own station plans. These are offered only as a guide. The examples are presented in sequential order and each plan requires approximately three and one-half hours for *full rotation of all station groups*. When using the laying the groundwork stations, the emphasis is placed on the students learning the seven basic skills stated above.

### Sample Plan/Laying the Groundwork: Phase One

This sample plan is for the first day.

***Station 1: "Broadcast News"***
The Sections of the Newspaper

***Learning Modes***
Practicing Skills and Putting It All Together

***Why This Station Is Important***
Students are introduced to:

1. Parts of the newspaper. The newspaper is one of the primary learning resources students use at this station.
2. The 5W's form. This serves as a planning guide and a reporting form.

***Student Group Instructions***
At this station, read and review the information in your section of the newspaper. Use the 5W's form to record information that is in your section of the newspaper. Remember, you are preparing for your news

broadcast. Do a thorough job *now,* so you will be ready to videotape in the next learning station plan.

Place your 5W's sheet in the quality finished product envelope. I will review it and return it to you so you can use it as your planning guide to put together your news broadcast.

### Station Goals
Students will learn about a section of the newspaper.

### SCANS Goals
Workplace competencies of acquiring, evaluating, interpreting, and communicating information; basic skills of writing, speaking, and listening; and thinking skills of thinking creatively and making decisions

### Station Equipment and Resource Materials
5W's form, clipboards, newspaper sections

### Student Materials
Pencil, notebook

### Station Happenings
Prior to using this station, as a whole-group activity, students were introduced to the different sections of the newspaper. Next, I presented the students with a newspaper section sign-up sheet. I instructed each table group to select two sections and to prioritize then as Choice #1 and Choice #2. Students have two days to enter their table's preferences.

Each group needs to talk about how the group is going to present its newspaper section: Is each person going to report on an item in that section? Is there a need to do work beyond the time the group has at the station? If more time is needed, students determine how much time they need to complete this report.

### Assessment and Accountability
A completed 5W's form in the quality finished product envelope

### Station 2: "How's It Going?"
Presentation Skills

### Learning Modes
Building Knowledge and Practicing Skills

### Why This Station Is Important
Students are introduced to:

1. Components of an effective presentation

2. Presentation assessment criteria forms

3. Notetaking format

### Student Group Instructions

At this station, we will talk about the key factors that go into setting the standards for making a quality presentation. We will use the English text and view a videotape that gives an example of an effective presentation.

Please bring your English notebook so you can take notes. In addition, I will share with you a presentation assessment form and we will discuss how this relates to your "Broadcast News" videotape presentation.

### Station Goals

Students will understand the key components of effective communication skills needed for a presentation. Students will become familiar with presentation assessment criteria.

### SCANS Goals

Workplace competencies of interpersonal skills and information acquisition; and basic skills of reading, writing, listening, and speaking

### Station Equipment and Resource Materials

Teacher-led discussion and presentation videotape

### Student Materials

English notebooks

### Student Examples

In the middle of the year, some students begin to see how their presentations improve when they use the assessment criteria as a guide for planning their presentation.

### Station Happenings

We discuss the skills that students will be working on when they put together a presentation. Students' initial reaction is sometimes one of confusion and they show an inability to make any connections between assessment and grades. Some really don't believe that they can assess other students or themselves. Their mindset is they do the work and the teacher tells them how they did with a grade or a comment.

Together, we view a short news report presentation, and students use the assessment form to learn more about the assessment process. In the beginning of the year we concentrate on the most simple presentation skills for assessment, such as eye contact, clarity, and articulation. Second-year students will have learned these skills and are now focusing on polishing their personal presentation styles.

### Assessment and Accountability

Short written or oral quiz, and accurate notes in notebook

### Station 3: Computer

The Menu Bar

*Learning Modes*
Building Knowledge and Practicing Skills

*Why This Station Is Important*
Students are introduced to:

1. Menu bar, font sizes, type styles
2. Use of the mouse while getting familiar with the word-processing program
3. Practice for the second-year students in being teachers
4. Use of the quality finished product envelope

*Student Group Instructions*
Please work in pairs on this activity. Use your observation (looking) skills for this activity. Use what you have learned about the word-processing program to create a new word-processing file. Use the mouse to click on "Format," which is located at the top of the screen. Look at your options. Experiment with font, size, and style. Do you remember how to do this? Drag the mouse down to the font choice and click on it. After you are familiar with the different fonts, sizes, and styles available to you, please key in the following message, experimenting with the fonts and variety of letter sizes and styles of your choice.

Writing Instructions: "Wrapping a Present"
By Ted Block and Mary Goode

Be sure to include everything in the message except you should insert your own names after the word "By." Save on your own disk or on the hard drive. Then print out your work and place the hard copy in the quality finished product envelope.

*Station Goals*
Introduction to the computer, print and format functions

*SCANS Goals*
Workplace competencies of information and technology; basic skills of writing; and thinking skills of using efficient learning techniques to acquire new skills

*Station Equipment and Resource Materials*
Computers and word-processing software

*Student Materials*
Station sheet/student disk

### Station Happenings
Students use hands-on experimentation to familiarize themselves with different fonts, sizes, and styles in the word-processing program. These same instructions can be applied to both introductory and more advanced word processing, databases, spreadsheets, and draw programs.

### Assessment and Accountability
Students print out a copy of their message.

### Station 4: Multimedia
Parts of Speech

### Learning Modes
Building Knowledge and Practicing Skills

### Why This Station Is Important
Students are introduced to a computer-management tool and students begin to practice assessing what they know.

### Student Group Instructions
Explore the *Wally Word Works* computer software by selecting the Definition option from the MAIN MENU. Review definitions for all parts of speech.

### Station Goals
Students will identify and use parts of speech (language arts) in a drill-and-practice game format on the computer.

### SCANS Goals
Basic skills of reading and following instructions

### Station Equipment and Resource Materials
A computer (Apple or IBM model) and *Wally Word Works* software. (Please see the computer disk that accompanies this book for details about *Wally Word Works.*)

### Student Materials
None

### Student Examples
The software-management system allows students to move on to work with other parts of speech, progressing at their own pace. Progress reports can be stored on the student's disk.

### Station Happenings
Students usually work in pairs to extend and practice their knowledge of adjectives, verbs, and nouns in a game format. This gives feedback and

practice while building their grammar skills. Later in the year, after conferring with the teacher, students using this program determine which parts and how many parts of speech they will practice.

### Assessment and Accountability
The program keeps track of students' work on the computer and can be stored on their own disk.

### Station 5: Experiential
Language Arts and Literature Check

### Learning Modes
Practicing Skills and Putting It All Together

### Why This Station Is Important
Students are introduced to:

1. The role of volunteers

2. Collaborative student efforts, which include feedback from fellow learners

### Student Group Instructions
At this station, Mrs. Jopp, Mary's mother, will be wrapping a present with you. Next, you and Mrs. Jopp will discuss the materials needed, the steps used for wrapping the present, and the specific kinds of words that facilitate the writing of instructions (such as *first, now, to begin with, last, next*, and *finally)*.These are called *time order words*. Please bring your English/Literature notebooks and a pencil.

After you have begun writing your own instructions, Mrs. Jopp will be checking with each of you to see if you know which fable you need to read this week and if you have the fable quiz criteria in the literature section of your notebook.

### Station Goals
Students will write out the steps involved in wrapping a present, focusing on the use of order vocabulary and descriptive instructional sequences.

### SCANS Goals
Basic skills of writing, and thinking skills of thinking creatively and reasoning

### Station Equipment and Resource Materials
Wrapping paper, bows, tape, tags, scissors, boxes with inexpensive presents in them, and *Macmillan English* teacher's manual. (Any standard English textbook offers many lessons that are very useable in the station format.)

### Student Materials
English/Literature notebooks and pencil

### Station Happenings
Students choose a gift box to wrap. With the assistance of a parent volunteer, they write down the steps involved in wrapping a present, using proper order vocabulary. They use higher-order thinking skills as they break down their instructions for gift wrapping into a step-by-step process. At the end of the station, they open their present.

### Assessment and Accountability
Students beginning attempts at gift-wrapping instructions are evaluated for logical order.

### Station 6: Multipurpose
Descriptive Words and Imagery

### Learning Mode
Building Knowledge

### Why This Station Is Important
Students are introduced to:

1. Use of the quality finished product envelope
2. Use of the tape recorder
3. Importance of reading *all* the station instructions before starting

### Student Group Instructions
Listen to the story, "I Hole Up in a Snowstorm," on the *Listening to Literature* audiotape. If you want to follow along with the story in the book, it begins on page 244. Listen for as many descriptive words (adjectives) as you can. Write these descriptive words in your English notebook.

After you have listened to the story, as a group, discuss and answer the questions on the tape. Note the quality standards for handing in completed papers. When you have finished, place your group's work in the quality finished product envelope. (Option: Students can word-process their answers. Laptops are useful for this activity.)

### Station Goals
The student will identify adjectives in a taped story and discuss the imagery used in the story. Students will answer comprehension questions about the story.

### SCANS Goals
Basic skills of reading, writing, and listening

### Station Equipment and Resource Materials
Tape player, tape, English books, computer

### Student Materials
English/Literature notebook and pencil

### Station Happenings
It's good to have a parent at this station in the beginning or to locate the station fairly close to you. Headphones are useful to minimize the noise.

### Assessment and Accountability
Groups complete the comprehension questions

## Sample Plan/Laying the Groundwork: Phase Two

This sample plan is for the second day.

### Station 1: "Broadcast News"
Learning about Your Newspaper

### Learning Modes
Practicing Skills and Putting It All Together

### Why This Station Is Important
Students will:

1. Learn to use the camcorder
2. Complete the 5W's form
3. Put together their first news broadcast

### Student Group Instructions
At this station, you will put together a news broadcast about your newspaper section. Videotape this with your group and try to keep the broadcast within four minutes. Remember to review your presentation criteria and to start your broadcast with introductions of your group and your newspaper section.

Practice using the correct pronunciation of words. When every group has taped, we will have a video covering all the sections of the newspaper.

Be *careful* with the camcorder and be *kind* to each other. Remember to leave the station as you found it. Is the newspaper picked up? Is the camcorder in its place and is the battery recharging? Where are the 5W's forms?

### Station Goals
Students will create a four-minute informational videotape on a section of the newspaper using good communication skills. They will practice col-

laborative skills, gain experience in planning a video sequence, and practice operating a video camera.

### SCANS Goals
Workplace competencies of using resources and time efficiently; interpersonal skills of working together as members of a team, information, and technology; basic skills of reading and speaking; thinking skills of reasoning and making decisions; and personal qualities of individual responsibility and sociability

### Station Equipment and Resource Materials
Daily newspaper, camcorder, videotape, 5W's form

### Student Materials
Pencils

### Station Happenings
As students gain experience in this weekly station activity, they begin to take the production more seriously and critique their finished product astutely to make future improvements.

### Assessment and Accountability
The videotape is the finished product.

### Station 2: "How's It Going?"
Writing Instructions

### Learning Mode
Practicing Skills

### Why This Station Is Important
Students become more accustomed to:

1. One-on-one help and talking with the teacher
2. Collaborative efforts and feedback from fellow students
3. Being accountable for work from another station.

### Student Group Instructions
We will read and review each person's writing instructions for "Wrapping a Present." Also, I will be checking your notes on writing instructions that you worked on with Mrs. Jopp.

### Station Goals
Students will review their gift-wrapping instructions and revise any unclear steps to improve their instructions.

### SCANS Goals

Thinking skills of making decisions and problem-solving; personal qualities of demonstrating understanding and politeness in group settings; and basic skills of listening and speaking with others and revising, editing and conferencing about writing

### Station Equipment and Resource Materials

Teacher

### Student Materials

English/Literature notebooks and pencils

### Station Happenings

Students get a chance to share their order and detail vocabulary with their group and to collaboratively help each other to improve their written instructions for gift-wrapping. It is very helpful for students to receive feedback from fellow students to improve any unclear or poorly written instructions.

### Assessment and Accountability

Teacher observation of student discussion and revised gift-wrapping instructions

### Station 3: Computer

Creating a Word-Processing File

### Learning Modes

Practicing Skills, Putting It All Together

### Why This Station Is Important

Students learn to:

1. Create a computer file.
2. Prepare their personal disk for use throughout the year.
3. Second-year students exercise teaching skills with first-year students.
4. Use the printer.

### Student Group Instructions

First-year students, write your name and class number on the label of the disk using a fine-point marker. Then initialize and name your disk on the computer. Next, create and save a file on your disk called "Writing Instructions." Use the EDIT function on the menu bar at the top of the screen. If you need a little review, what are two resources easily available to you? Explore the cut and paste functions using your writing instructions.

Print out your work, if you would like to share this with me. Second-year students, I would appreciate you helping first-year students if they need help initializing the disks.

If you have time, begin to key in your instructions for "Wrapping a Present." Did you save it? What is the name of your file?

### Station Goals
Students will word-process their gift-wrapping instructions. They will review the file creation process and experiment with the cut and paste function.

### SCANS Goals
Workplace competencies of technology and information; basic skills of reading and writing

### Station Equipment and Resource Materials
Computers, word-processing program, software instruction booklet

### Student Materials
Student's written gift-wrapping instructions, disks

### Station Happenings
Students work in pairs to enter their word-processing document and to experiment with cut and paste functions. Second-year students pair up with first-year students for this activity and act as mentors because of their familiarity with the computer.

### Assessment and Accountability
Initialized disk and a new file created; word-processed instructions

### Station 4: Multimedia
Parts of Speech

### Learning Modes
Building Knowledge and Practicing Skills

### Why This Station Is Important
Students become accustomed to the student progress chart, a management aspect of software.

### Student Group Instructions
You will be learning how to use the progress chart of this program. Your station group trainer will be instructing you. Please work in pairs and print out one of your exercises in which you identified adjectives, nouns, and verbs using the progress chart of *Wally Word Works*.

If you do not have a printer, please raise your hand when you are ready to show me the screen that shows your progress. If you feel you are ready to practice with more parts of speech, read the software instructional booklet to find out how. Start with the Table of Contents.

### Station Goals
The student will learn to use the student progress records for feedback and to evaluate how they are doing.

### SCANS Goals
Workplace skills of acquiring data, and basic skills of reading and writing

### Station Equipment and Resource Material
Computer and Wally Word Works (printer optional)

### Student Materials
None

### Station Happenings
Students will use the *Wally Word Works* software program and then access the student progress chart to see how they are doing. The progress chart is useful for immediate feedback and seems to motivate the students to accomplish more learning.

### Assessment and Accountability
Either a printout of the student progress chart or a teacher check of the progress chart results on the computer screen.

### Station 5: Experiential
Choice—Self-Directed Learning

### Learning Mode
Practicing Skills

### Why This Station Is Important
Students are introduced to:

1. A method of dealing with individual rates of learning
2. Self-management

### Student Group Instructions
Check to see if you need to work on any of these items: "Wrapping a Present" instructions, M & M skills (see Chapter 7), spelling work, or reading in our whole-group discussion book, *Sarah Plain and Tall.*

### Station Goals
Students will use the time wisely to work on any class assignments that have not been completed.

### SCANS Goals
Workplace competencies of allocating time; thinking skills of making decisions; and the personal quality of self-management

### Station Equipment and Resource Materials
A variety of educational activities and settings

### Student Materials
Whatever they need to accomplish the task they have decided to work on

### Station Happenings
Students choose the activity they most need to accomplish at this station. Students develop the skills of time management and prioritizing work while they develop a sense of self-direction and accomplishment.

### Assessment and Accountability
Students who do not choose to work are usually quite visible to me or other students in the group. Between peer pressure and teacher encouragement, students learn to keep on task.

### Station 6: Multipurpose
American History

### Learning Mode
Building Knowledge and Practicing Skills

### Why This Station Is Important
Students are introduced to:

1. Good viewing habit guidelines
2. Developing individual responsibility and self-discipline without the teacher's direct supervision.

### Student Group Instructions
Collette, Austin's mom, will be sitting with you to observe your great viewing habits when you watch the video titled *Native Americans: The History of a People.*

Before you start the video, please review the study sheet with Collette to further prepare yourselves for the video. As you watch the video, take notes on any information that you think will be important for your Native-American project work that we will be starting soon. Remember, this is one way of building your knowledge base for starting your Native-American project work.

### Station Goals
Students will get a sense of the cultural diversity of Native Americans and a brief history of the conflict between Native Americans and European settlers.

*SCANS Goals*
Basic skills of listening and writing, and thinking skills of using learning techniques to acquire new knowledge

*Station Equipment and Resource Materials*
VCR and monitor, videotape, and laptop word processor (If you have a laptop available, this is a perfect student motivator for good notetaking.)

*Student Materials*
Social studies notebooks and pencils

*Station Happenings*
Students view a videotape and focus on important information they want to write down in their social studies notebooks. We often view a video-tape twice to increase students' learning opportunities and comprehension. The first time we view the videotape as a whole group and the second time students view it at a station.

*Assessment and Accountability*
Student notes in social studies notebooks

### Sample Plan/Laying the Groundwork: Phase Three

This sample plan is for the third day.

*Station 1: "Broadcast News"*
Following Written Instructions

*Learning Mode*
Putting It All Together

*Why This Station Is Important*
Students are:

> 1. Practicing assessment of individual and group work
> 2. Experiencing the importance of meeting deadlines

*Student Group Instructions*
Since everyone decided to make a "Wrapping a Present/Following Instructions" videotape, you will have an opportunity to do this today. These are the criteria you must follow: Demonstrate wrapping a present following one student's written instructions. A rehearsal is imperative to producing a quality presentation. (Be ready to tell me what *imperative* means.)

*Station Goals*
Students will produce a videotape following a clearly written set of directions for wrapping a present.

### SCANS Goals
Basic skills of reading and speaking; thinking skills of reasoning and making decisions; and personal qualities of responsibility and sociability

### Station Equipment and Resource Materials
VCR and camcorder, videotape, gift boxes, wrapping paper, tape, scissors, bows, gift tags, and inexpensive gifts

### Student Materials
Written student gift-wrapping instructions

### Station Happenings
Students will choose the best example of gift-wrapping instructions written by a group member and use it to videotape a demonstration.

### Assessment and Accountability
Gift-wrapping demonstration videotape

### Station 2: "How's It Going?"
Critique Your Newspaper Video

### Learning Mode
Practicing Skills

### Why This Station Is Important
Students use:

1. Assessment forms
2. Conversation and collaborative efforts with teacher guidance and feedback for peer evaluation

### Student Group Instructions
At this station, we will view, discuss, and assess your *Learning about Your Newspaper* videotape. We will discuss the following questions: Did your group meet the criteria? Do you want to do it again or keep it as it is? Why or why not? Do you want to make revision plans?

### Station Goals
Student groups will evaluate their newspaper videotape.

### SCANS Goals
Workplace competencies of resource skills of evaluating performance and providing feedback, and thinking skills of reasoning and making decisions

### Station Equipment and Resource Materials
VCR and videotapes

### Student Materials
Paper and pencil, assessment criteria sheets

### Student Examples
Students will make observations. For example, one group was not pleased with the way one member was chewing gum while talking on the tape. They decided to make a rule that there would be no gum chewing in future videotapes. Another group felt a group member was talking too fast and suggested that they work on slowing down their speech in the next videotape.

### Station Happenings
Students take a critical look at the videotape of their newspaper section. They consider all of the elements of the presentation, including technical aspects like wiggling the camera too much, background noise, and lighting. Personal performance qualities, such as eye contact and talking too fast, are also taken into consideration. The group makes decisions on how to improve their final videotape.

### Assessment and Accountability
Students' comments about the *Learning about Your Newspaper* videotape

### Station 3: Computer
Word Processing

### Learning Mode
Practicing Skills

### Why This Station Is Important
Students become familiar with word processing as they word-process their final draft of instructions.

### Student Group Instructions
Insert your disk and call up the file needed for word processing your "Writing Instructions for Wrapping a Present." Remember to keep all copies of your writing instructions in your writing folder. Eventually, these will be stapled together with your final copy on top.

Try to use everything you have learned about word-processing features to make your work as easy as possible. When you finish, save your work, print out a copy, and put it into the quality finished product envelope.

### Station Goals
Students will word-process their final draft of gift-wrapping instructions.

### SCANS Goals
Workplace competencies of applying technology to specific tasks, and basic skills of writing

### Station Equipment and Resource Materials
Computers, word-processing program, printer, and paper

### Student Materials
Gift-wrapping written instructions and  student disks

### Station Happenings
Students will create their own format, such as boldface letters for the title, for entering the gift-wrapping instructions.

### Assessment and Accountability
Printed copy of students' gift-wrapping instructions

### Station 4: Wally Word Works
Practice and Progress Check

### Learning Mode
Practicing Skills

### Why This Station Is Important
Students practice using:

1. The printer
2. The quality finished product envelope
3. Self-assessment and decision-making skills

### Student Group Instructions
Use *Wally Word* to continue learning about the parts of speech. Before you leave this station, make a hard copy of your progress chart and place it in the quality finished product envelope. Would you like to include *Wally Word Works* as one of the learning activities at a choice station?

### Station Goals
Students will practice using different parts of speech. They will assess which parts of speech they have mastered.

### SCANS Goals
Basic skills of writing

### Station Equipment and Resource Materials
Computer, *Wally Word Works,* printer, and paper

### Student Materials
None

### Station Happenings
Students are given the opportunity to make the decision of whether they are going to print out the parts of speech definitions for their own use. Also, the students continue to assess how well they have learned the parts. They use their progress chart to help them make this assessment.

### Assessment and Accountability
Record of student progress

### Station 5: Science
Sorting Lego Kits

### Learning Mode
Practicing Skills

### Why This Station Is Important
Students get acquainted with all of the Lego building pieces, including wires, motors, gears, axles, weights, touch sensors, and light sensors.

### Student Group Instructions
Select a partner and choose a Lego kit to sort and organize according to the colored chart provided. Set aside any broken pieces, gears, or rubber binders so that replacements can be ordered. Ms. Juliani will be at this station to assist you. Remember we are sorting, not building.

### Station Goals
Students must sort the Lego pieces according to the diagram and familiarize themselves with the Lego components.

### SCANS Goals
Workplace competencies of caring for resources; thinking skills of reasoning; and personal qualities of individual responsibility

### Station Equipment and Resource Materials
Legos and storage containers, layout diagram

### Student Materials
None

### Station Happenings
Students work cooperatively to sort the pieces into the proper place in the storage container. Each group decides which process to use in order to share the responsibility equally. This activity also helps build student awareness of the different Lego pieces and the importance of proper storage. Legos provide hands-on learning about physical science concepts such as understanding mechanical advantage.

### Assessment and Accountability
Correctly sorted Lego containers

### Station 6: Multipurpose
Organization and Self-Management

### Learning Mode
Putting It All Together

### Why This Station Is Important
Students can see:

1. How well they have applied earlier lessons on organizing their notebooks

2. How organization and accountability are crucial to station use

### Student Group Instructions
At this station, Mrs. Maki, Tom's mother, will be here to check that you have the following materials and that they are divided and labeled appropriately:

1. Assignment notebook

2. Social and Science notebook

3. English and Literature notebook

4. Classroom expectations and procedures notebook

5. M + M folder

6. Spelling notebook and *Aesop's Fables* quiz book

If you need to make your writing folder or logo planning booklet there are written instructions available to you. Making a sketch book is optional. Mrs. Maki will give you further details and provide you with assistance as needed.

### Station Goals
Students will demonstrate that they have followed directions and have the appropriately labeled learning materials for the classroom.

### SCANS Goals
Workplace competencies of organizing materials; thinking skills of the ability to learn; and personal qualities of individual responsibility and self-management.

### Station Equipment and Resource Materials
Spreadsheet and parent volunteer

*Student Materials*

1. Assignment notebook
2. Social and Science notebook
3. English and Literature notebook
4. Classroom expectations and procedures notebook
5. M + M folder
6. Spelling notebook and *Aesop's Fables* quiz book

*Student Examples*

The most frequent problem at this station is with first-year students who do not understand how to use the assignment notebook. Also, others may not have labeled their notebooks properly.

*Station Happenings*

It is very important that students learn organizational skills. Proper training at the beginning of the year facilitates learning and eliminates student frustration. Students with few organizational skills are assisted in learning these skills by observing fellow learners in the classroom.

I sometimes assist at this station to help with notebook organization. (Option: Second-year students may produce a short instructional videotape on effective organization and use of assignment notebooks.)

*Assessment and Accountability*

An electronic spreadsheet is used for checking off each student when they meet the criteria.

## CHOICE LEARNING STATION

### Description

The primary functions of the choice learning station are to provide time for students to work on any unfinished task or to choose what they want to work on. When students first use this station, teacher guidance and feedback is needed in order to help students:

1. Reflect on unfinished work.
2. Decide work priorities.
3. Plan for needed resources.

This station is a practicing ground for students to use decision-making and self-management skills.

For the teacher who is just starting to use learning stations, the choice station is helpful for several reasons. If you are unsure of how to gauge the time needed for some stations, using a choice learning station will allow flexibility for different work styles and rates. Also, if you are short on equipment, a choice station offers students various activities to work on while waiting to use equipment.

Finally, this is an excellent opportunity for you to guide students in planning and making decisions. The choice learning station provides the opportunity to conference briefly with a student about incomplete work.

### Training for This Station

During the first month, we discuss, in whole group, activities that students may work on at a choice station. Perhaps one student states he needs to work on his discussion book summary. Either a student or I write this on the blackboard or enter this on the computer and display it on a large monitor. We continue until all their activities are listed. I may remind students of any activities that may be coming due, such as Junior Great Books discussions. It also gives me a chance to ask who has a book conference with me and to check whether they are prepared.

After we compile our list, we read it over together. After a month or so, students usually know what they need to do during this time, and the whole group activity of compiling a list of activities is no longer necessary. The following list is a sample of a choice station activities.

### List of Choice Station Activities

Check if you need to finish any of the following:

- Your Mother's Day card
- Math work to meet your math goal for tomorrow
- Literature book presentation
- Spelling
- Crystals experiment
- Power vs. speed Lego models
- Word-processing stories
- Individual writing work
- Small-group Lego work
- Complete "Broadcast News" videotape

### Including the Choice Station in the Multisubject Learning-Station Plan

You can include the choice station in any learning-station plan and at any time. I include the choice station at least once or twice every two weeks, usually in the multisubject learning-station plan. I most often use Station

6, multipurpose, as the choice station. Eventually, students sense when a choice learning station is needed and will ask to have it included in the plan. The choice station serves nicely as a back-up station when a parent cancels plans to help at a learning station or when equipment does not work.

# PROJECT LEARNING STATIONS

## Description

Both individual and group-project work, sometimes referred to as *theme learning,* is a common learning technique in my classroom. Project work incorporates all disciplines into a single theme. Projects create many opportunities for students to practice SCANS skills and competencies. These projects involve all of the three learning modes of (1) building a knowledge base, (2) practicing and applying skills, and (3) putting it all together.

The putting-it-all-together mode in project work is a good example of what some educators define as students producing their own knowledge about a topic. In addition, projects involve multisensory, interdisciplinary, and performance learning. Best of all, the students like it and they work hard.

To ensure that this third learning mode happens, I design the first set of station plans around building the students' knowledge base. In doing so, students are then better equipped for more in-depth learning activities such as writing a research report or business letter.

The learning-station format is flexible enough to let me extend station time when needed or to regroup equipment to suit a particular phase of the project. The learning-station structure also helps students develop constructive and creative projects and gives me the opportunity to provide the necessary directions students need when working on projects.

(*Note:* Sometimes there may be a few students who do not like group-project work. Most often, I allow students the option of working alone if they prefer.)

## Training for Project Stations

I start project learning stations after the whole group has been trained to use the learning-station concept. I introduce project learning with well-defined requirements. The first step is to present the Project Requirements List (see Figure 5.1) and the project learning-station plan to the whole group. We review project guidelines, planning strategies, and standards. Then we form our project learning groups.

**FIGURE 5.1    Project Requirement List: Topic—Native Americans**

- Whole-Group Timeline—a few entries about your Native-American group
- Maps showing where your Native-American group lives—one computer-generated and one free-hand drawing map
- Shelter model
- Craft and artifacts samples
- Vocabulary words illustrated related to your Native-American group (database entries optional)
- Teaching and learning activity designed by your group
- Outline from text about your Native-American group
- Research report
- Business letter (Such as to the Bureau of Indian Affairs)
- Food, music, art representative of your Native-American group
- Animals and plants native to your Native-American group

At the "How's it going?" station, I explain and discuss again each of these requirements in detail and answer questions. During this time, students usually take notes to get specific project ideas and directions.

Also, because of the tendency for initial chaos with project work and the increased student activity and movement, I emphasize the importance of respecting co-workers, materials, and equipment. This means putting materials back, not wasting them, waiting your turn, and being prepared to use equipment. As students develop more expertise in doing projects, they have more input in designing their project work.

### Designing the Project Learning-Station Plan

There are a number of ways to design the project learning-station plan. One way is to use all the stations for project work. Included here is an example that shows how different parts of the Native-American project requirements have been divided among all six stations. The focus for all stations in this learning-station plan is to build motivation and interest, and to expose students to the many different resources available for their projects.

### Sample Plan/Project Learning Stations: Phase One

Topic: Native Americans

### Station 1: Broadcast News
### Student Group Instructions
At this station, please view and examine Native-American artifacts and learning resources displayed on the table. Make note of any *Cobblestone* or

*National Geographic* articles that will relate to your Native-American group. (Students use the *Cobblestone* or *National Geographic Index* to locate resources.)

### Station 2: "How's It Going?"
#### Student Group Instructions

At this station, I will explain in detail each of the Native American project requirements.

### Station 3: Computer
#### Student Group Instructions

Identify the location of the Native-American group you have chosen and prepare a map to illustrate where that group lives. You may decide as a group how you want to do this. There should be enough computers for you to pair up to explore the map-making capabilities of the *Hello* program. (See Chapter 6 for further details about the *Hello* program.) For example, if you have the Southwest Native Americans, indicate the states and portion of states that this group lives in. You may find your social studies text or the electronic encyclopedia helpful.

### Station 4: Multimedia
#### Student Group Instructions

Please use two computers to explore the Animal or Climate databases to gather more information about your group. You may want to take notes to use for your project work.

### Station 5: Experiential
#### Student Group Instructions

You will be learning about the basic parts of a business letter for the purpose of requesting information relating to your project. Mrs. Thomas will give you specific instructions when you get to this station.

### Station 6: Multipurpose
#### Student Group Instructions

This is your group planning time for your Native-American project. You also may use the *Groliers Encyclopedia* on the CD-ROM disk to explore information that might be useful for your research.

## Decreasing the Number of Project Learning Stations

Another way I design project stations to give a longer time for project work is to combine two groups per station making a station group size of eight or nine students. With two groups per station, we now have three stations on our learning-station plan instead of six, and we have doubled the station time at each station. This is a comfortable group size for discussion at a station. Everyone gets a chance to ask questions and take part in the conversation.

### Sample Plan/Project Learning Stations: Phase Two

Topic: Native Americans

### Station 1: "Broadcast News" (Independent Group Project Work)
### Learning Modes
Building Knowledge, Practicing Skills, and Putting It All Together

### Student Group Instructions
You will have 45 minutes to work on your projects. All equipment and resource materials are available for your use. Mrs. Marks and Tom will be available as resource people if you have project or general research questions.

If you are working on your group's business letter, there are a few samples of quality business letters posted at the computers. Use them for a reference if you need to. Before you print this letter, please have someone from your group proofread your final draft on the desktop.

### Station 2: "How's It Going?" (Project Work)

### Learning Modes
Building Knowledge and Practicing Skills

### Student Group Instructions
At this station, we will review your groups' project plans and discuss any work you may have started.

### Station 3: Multipurpose (Guest Speaker)
### Learning Mode
Building Knowledge and Putting It All Together

### Student Group Instructions
At this station, Mr. Naquinabe, a Native American, will speak to you about his life. He has beautiful artifacts and authentic stories to share with you. Absorb everything you can and feel free to take notes.

This station provides you with another opportunity to practice communication skills such as discussing, sharing ideas, and learning how to explore and gather information about a topic through effective questioning techniques.

### Including Project Learning into Multisubject Learning-Station Plan

When integrating the project stations into the multisubject station plans, I designate two stations—usually multimedia and multipurpose—for project work. I repeat these stations until projects are completed.

During project station work, I am always working on quality control. Students are interested and motivated to do quality work. However, in the beginning of project learning, a great deal of teacher guidance is required in order for students to learn how to achieve quality work and to realize that persistence is crucial.

## TEST-TAKING LEARNING STATIONS

At the beginning of the year, I design a multisubject learning-station plan using four stations, with one of these stations designated for test taking. Test taking takes place at the "How's it going?" station. When designing this station plan, my primary considerations are to minimize student movement and noise level, and to allow for teacher guidance at the testing station.

I made the change from administering tests to a whole group to small groups for several reasons. First, I rethought the whole concept of testing. If tests are to reflect what students have learned, the test itself must be designed to give students the opportunity to do so. For example, if I want to know if students can actually measure the dimensions of an object, the test should actually provide the student with the opportunity to demonstrate this knowledge and skill. A multiple-choice test does not always do this.

The station structure accommodates this kind of hands-on testing as well as other assessment methods that are virtually impossible in large-group testing. I use a variety of test methods with my students, including traditional tests, hands-on concepts demonstration, essay writing tests, and final presentations on a topic or a tangible product. Another advantage of test taking at a station is that I am able to help students build test-taking skills and to answer any questions they may have in a fairly risk-free setting.

The third advantage is that stations are extremely flexible. The time allotment for these stations is still 30 minutes but those students who finish early are able to move to one of the other three stations or to return to their seats to continue independent work. For those students who need more time, the station format allows them to remain at this station. An underlying advantage of this flexibility is that it gives students control and teaches them how to pace themselves. For example, in some instances students need a break during a test and are able to take one at this station. After a few months into the school year, when students have established a few basic test-taking strategies, I may increase the size of the station group.

### Sample Plan/Test-Taking Learning Stations

#### Station 1: "Broadcast News"
Hands-On Science Testing (Performance Based)

*Learning Mode*
Putting It All Together

*Student Group Instructions*
The performance assessment task at this station is for you to create two Lego models (using gears, etc.), building (1) for speed and (2) for power. Then explain what you did in this experiment and what physical science concepts are operating in this experiment.

*Station Happenings*
Two volunteers are needed for this station. Both volunteers in different rooms (sometimes in a hallway) videotape one child at a time from the station group. Next, the student explains his or her experiment, identifies parts needed, and shares any insights or questions he or she might have concerning this experiment. This task takes each student about 10 minutes to complete. The videotape is used for assessment.

*Station 2: "How's It Going?"*
Standard Science Test from Science Series

*Learning Mode*
Putting It All Together

*Student Group Instructions*
At this station, we will be taking the science test and practicing effective test-taking strategies.

*Station 3: Computers*
Word-Processing Final Draft

*Learning Modes*
Practicing Skills and Putting It All Together

*Student Group Instructions*
At this station, I would like each of you to enter the final draft of your story on the word-processing file called *Our Book.*

*Station 4: Multipurpose*
Choice

*Learning Modes*
Building Knowledge, Practicing Skills, and Putting It All Together

*Student Group Instructions*
At this station, you may work on any assignments that you need to finish. Tomorrow is Friday. Is your homework packet finished? Check your assignment notebook to see how you are doing on things. There is a

choice chart with a list of several magazines just waiting for you to investigate and peruse (read) their offerings.

## PRESENTATION REHEARSAL LEARNING STATIONS

### Description

Like the projects stations, the presentation rehearsal stations use interdisciplinary learning with an emphasis on creating a product. These products can be written, oral, models, or videotape presentations. We do presentations on a regular basis in our class.

For example, as a culmination of our Native-American project, a small group may present all of the information it has compiled. At other times, students may present poems they have written or demonstrate a new computer program. Final presentations are given to other class members, given to other classes, or videotaped for taking home or for Parent Night.

These presentation rehearsal stations are designed to prepare students for presentations. I have found it most effective to locate these stations with me or with a parent volunteer who is skilled at and comfortable with making last-minute revisions and corrections. This provides effective direction and minimizes last-minute chaos. Students feel much more comfortable with this small-group station format, especially when they are giving individual presentations.

A few days before a presentation, I will include two or three stations for presentation rehearsal in the multisubject station learning plan. Shown here is an example of how I have used these stations in preparation for Parent Night. (See Chapter 7 for further details about Parent Night.)

### Sample Plan/Presentation Rehearsal Learning Stations

**Station 1: "Broadcast News"**
Lego Model Videotape

**Student Group Instructions**
At this station, get your Lego model and your short explanation speech ready for videotaping. Then videotape. Does three minutes sound long enough for each of you? If you need more time for taping, please let me know.

**Station 2: "How's It Going?"**
Parent Night Preparation

**Student Group Instructions**
Be ready, as a group, to share your overall presentation plan. Reminder: Parent Night is on Tuesday, March 31st at 7:00 P.M.

### *Station 3: Computer*
Parent Night Preparation

### *Student Group Instructions*
Use this station for any last-minute Parent Night preparation requiring computer use.

### *Station 4: Multimedia*
Science/Language Arts

### *Student Group Instructions*
At this station, please continue with your group's next lesson in the weather unit. Check that you have your materials and the remote. Decide on a fair way to handle the use of the remote control for operating the laser disk player. When you are finished using the laser disk and have completed the "On Your Own" section in your weather booklet, let me know. I will review this section with each of you. Please remember the procedure for leaving this station. Thank you.

### *Station 5: Experiential*
Language Arts/Presentation Preparation

### *Student Group Instructions*
I have listed the parts of your presentation.

1. Summary
2. Acrostic poem
3. Important facts and words board
4. Map
5. Illustrations
6. Models

Look over every single letter, word, and so on very carefully. Practice what you are going to say if you have time.

### *Station 6: Multipurpose*
"Broadcast News" Videotape Selections

### *Student Group Instructions*
View and evaluate past "Broadcast News" videotapes. What do you need for this station? Please select one "Broadcast News" that we can show for Parent Night.

## ART AND CULTURE LEARNING STATIONS

Once or twice a month, I use art and culture stations as a complete learning station plan that we complete in one full day. Depending on the station content and help available, I use four to six stations. Instead of my working at the "How's it going?" station, I rotate among different station groups to read with them, observe, and discuss interesting facts related to the specific station. I also like to use a volunteer to ensure smooth running of these stations. The following is a sample station plan for art and culture activities.

### Sample Station Plan/Art and Culture Learning Stations

Theme: Native Americans

### Station 1: Sand Painting
### Student Group Instructions
Begin this station by reading a short magazine article with details about how sand paintings were used by Navaho Indians to cure illness or lift a curse. Review the steps in the sand-painting process which are illustrated to help you create your own painting.

### Station 2: Being a Creative Weaver
### Student Group Instructions
At this station, you will read about weaving terminology—such as warp and texture—from the textbook lesson. Next, choose your yarn from the collection of varying textures and colors to make your twig weaving. How about hanging these in our room later? Refer to the lesson if you need to.

### Station 3: Prehistoric Agriculture
### Student Group Instructions
At this station, please take a few minutes to view the videotape on Native-American agriculture and its dramatic effect on the rise of civilization. Learn the story about corn, beans, and squash, and the intercropping techniques used to plant their gardens. Next, plant your garden using the intercropping techniques. The sample garden and the materials you'll need are available at the station exhibits.

### Station 4: Wampum Belt
### Student Group Instructions
At this station, you will read about how the Eastern Woodland group used seashells to make small beads called *wampum.* After you have read this information, each of you try to re-create the wampum belt pictured on the informational sheet. There are beading books and different kinds of beading looms for you to look at.

*Station 5: Keepers of the Earth—Audiotape*
*Student Group Instructions*

At this station, please put on headphones and, as a group, choose two stories from the tape to listen to. If you want to sketch or take notes on anything of interest to you, please do so.

*Station 6: You're Invited to a Dinner Party*
*Student Group Instructions*

Please read the lesson in the *Art in Action* textbook. Examine a variety of Native-American border patterns and designs and discuss common elements. Design your own pattern on a paper plate or placemat.

### Including Art and Culture Stations in Math or Multisubject Learning-Station Plans

Here are several examples of how art and culture stations can be integrated into other math and multisubject station plans:

- Students primarily use their graphing skills when they re-create the wampum belt at a manipulative station in a math-station plan.

- Another Native-American (Sioux) cultural activity for the math manipulative station is making dream catchers. These provide great opportunities for measurement skills and math applications.

- Another example is integrating a cooking station called "Wartime Food" into a World War II theme multisubject station plan. There is usually a parent at this station to read an informational article with the students and then to oversee the cooking and baking.

- Students can use the word-processing station to describe the food, games, music, and other entertainment of the 1920s as part of a multisubject station.

- Along with a *Cobblestone* article about the history of stenciling, a multisubject station could incorporate a hands-on stenciling experience. (*Cobblestone* is a history magazine that provides a complete curriculum in any topic that it covers and it is a very integral part of our history, art, and culture learning.)

## WRAP-UP ON LEARNING STATIONS

John Nesbitt coined the phrase *high-tech/high-touch* in his book titled *Megatrends*. Here, I use it to mean applying educational technologies (high-tech) to foster kindness, respect, and dignity while working with the mind, body, spirit, and heart of a child (high-touch). As educators, we know that this is an idealistic goal; however, I am convinced that learning stations make this a realistic one. Learning stations can be a major vehicle for acheiving a high-tech/high-touch balance in children's learning. Learning stations allow for creating an environment that is responsive to change. For example, time, space, furnishings, and equipment now become flexible *resources* rather than the *constraining factors* we are used to.

# chapter

# 6

# Technology Component

"Technology can be used to enslave people, to program them, to dehumanize them; or in a liberatory manner, to extend creativity and expressivity, to foster conviviality." (From "The Computer as a Convivial Tool," by Aaron Falbel, in *Constructionism*.) It is what people do with different technologies or tools, not what the tool is doing to them, that is important. We need to picture the computer as a convivial tool—one that enhances a person's freedom and autonomy, and one that is easily accessible and readily available.

If you use parent and community involvement with high-technology applications in the classroom, it can free up time to reward individual initiative and to give the personal attention that is so needed in a child's learning. There's no quick way to learn how to use technology. It is easy to *look* good using technology, but to *be good* at integrating technology requires a different learning perspective and a meaningful change on the part of the teacher.

Educational technology, when used appropriately, is a great instructional ally for the teacher and a great learning tool for students. It has the potential to double or triple your interaction time with students. It allows you to blend the best of your traditional teaching techniques with common-sense technology applications to create new and better learning synergies. However, even though technology can play a vital role in education, there is a reluctance to incorporate it into the classroom. Ivan Illich, philosopher and social critic, has made the following observation regarding technology: "The nonspecialist is discouraged from figuring out what makes a watch tick, or a telephone ring, or an electric typewriter work, by being warned that it will break if he tries. He can be told how a transistor radio works but he cannot find out for himself. This type of design tends to reinforce a noninventive society in which the experts find it progressively easier to hide behind their *expertise* and *beyond evaluation"* (*Deschooling Society*, 1971, p. 115). This prevailing attitude is the exact reason why we must use technologies in the classroom. We want to encourage innovation, curiosity, and assessment. We want our students to be their own experts.

This chapter is not intended to train you in how to use a computer, operate a camcorder, or run any of the other technologies that will be discussed. Rather, it is intended to help you see the potential for incorporating technology into classroom learning. Along with a description of each piece of technology, you will find examples that illustrate ideas for their uses in at least one of three of the following learning settings:

1. Learning station
2. Whole group
3. Individual

The types of learning modes and instructional settings will vary according to how you use the hardware and software.

## THE TECHNOLOGIES

The technologies and software that I will discuss are computers, telecommunications, supplementary software, integrated learning systems, laser disk players, CD-ROM players, camcorders, VCRs, audiotapes, and multimedia.

### Computers

#### Description
Computers include a central processing unit (brain), memory storage, monitor, keyboard, and other peripherals that perform programmed applications such as word processing. The software that I describe can be used with almost all brands of computers. Most of the software that I talk about in this section can be used in the following ways: on a network, at learning stations, for the whole group, in lab situations, or assigned for use at home.

#### How It Is Used
In my classroom, the primary reason for any hands-on learning tool is that it allows learning the *how* by doing. Students usually use computers in the following ways: word processing, spreadsheets and databases, Logo, telecommunications, problem solving, and skills practice. The amount of time for each of these fluctuates. In the beginning, we often used the computer for skills practice; now, skills practice receives the lowest usage,

mainly because I found students build their skills more effectively through other technologies, such as the videodisc or a CD-ROM disk. Students can acquire new skills as they use computer networks, CD-ROM disks, and multimedia.

Computer network use is growing. A network—a group of computers linked by hardware and software so that they can share information— offers a number of benefits, including ease of communication between users, sharing of software and peripheral devices, centralized management (less time spent loading disks), and instant access to files from other sites.

### Examples

**Word Processing**    Word processing is one of the major uses for our computers. My class uses a word-processing program for writing in all subject areas. The ease of revision and editing frees students to be more expressive, to write more, and, finally, to want to persevere at producing quality writing. This helps develop clear thinking skills. It gives me the time to have writing conferences with individual students, where we cannot only work on language mechanics but also focus our discussions on content and style. The students themselves use the editing features of the word-processing program to refine language mechanics and to experiment with sentence and word groupings on their own in a comfortable and relaxed manner.

**Databases**    Databases are collections of organized information (data). I use *Bank Street School Filer*, an introductory database program, and other ready-made databases to introduce the database concept and give students experience with how to use database files. As their database skills improve, the students become more capable at doing research and using databases to build their knowledge in different content areas.

Next, we create our own database to record classroom information such as student profiles, book recommendations, and miscellaneous categories, including a baseball card database. When students create these

### FIGURE 6.1   Book Recommendations Database

(The Book Recommendations Database is created by the whole group at a class meeting.)

This book database illustrates the information that is collected when a student makes an entry on the book database.

Book title
Author/Illustrator of the book
Type of literature
Setting of the book
Book recommendation
Interesting insights or events from the book

databases, they use database applications software such as *Microsoft or Clarisworks*. Students continue creating and using databases to collect, organize, and locate information. They develop thinking skills as they become proficient database users. Figure 6.1 provides an example of a Book Recommendations Database.

***Spreadsheets*** Spreadsheets are used for recordkeeping and classroom management tasks. Specific examples include:

- Goal-setting conference forms
- Decorative Can business inventory and sales
- Records of students' station work
- Observation checklists
- Students' math goals
- Weekly progress reports of student learning activities

***Logo*** Logo is a computer software disk that is made for just about all brands of computers. It is a programming language and an educational philosophy. It is discovery learning for students where *they can make* the connection between abstract reasoning and the actual experience. For example, making a square used to mean memorizing a formula; with Logo, making a square means conceptualizing the composition of the square. Logo is learning by doing; it creates a world of idea sharing and culture building. Students achieve problem solving using Logo.

In order for you and your students to realize the full potential of Logo, I strongly suggest you get a minimum of 20 hours in Logo training and maintain ongoing support. These are a few ways that I use Logo:

1. To problem-solve at math stations
2. To program Lego inventions (see Lego/Logo later in this chapter)
3. To construct projects
4. To use during choice time (see Chapter 7)

First-year students learn the basics of Logo through a once-a-week, 20-minute, teacher-led instruction. Students practice the new concepts at the problem-solving station. They have another opportunity to advance Logo skills through weekly mini-skill competency lessons (discussed in Chapter 3). Students start out working in pairs and share a disk but soon choose to have their own Logo disk.

These are some examples of ways students integrate Logo throughout the curriculum:

- One student constructed a Norwegian flag using Logo. He was able to share his programming procedures with the whole class.

- Another student, who had difficulty understanding the difference between acute and obtuse angles, decided to construct these angles using Logo.

Our next adventure will be to use electronic-mail with a school in St. Paul, Minnesota, to do some Logo sharing and troubleshooting.

*Lego/Logo*  Lego/Logo creates an environment for learning where the operating principles are initiative and freedom. Lego/Logo includes a computer disk; a construction kit containing Lego blocks, gears, wheels, electric motors and wires, and other building materials for students to build inventions; and an interface box that connects the computer to the Lego models. Using the Logo disk, they develop a program so their inventions can be computer-driven.

The following is a list of some uses for Lego/Logo:

- At learning stations, students can get hands-on experience with a physical science concept, such as different types of motion, by using Legos to build models. To illustrate the initiative and freedom that can happen with Lego learning, a group of girls, after building models of different types of motion, expanded the project on their own initiative by adding motors to them.
- In learning enhancement classes, students built a lift bridge from Legos and then created a Logo program to operate the lift bridge. (See Chapter 7 for a description of learning enhancement classes.)
- In project learning, students constructed a pyramid from Legos as part of a Mayan project.
- During Choice Time, students might choose to do individual or small-group Lego work.

As with Logo, the learning value of Lego depends on your getting good training, maintaining ongoing support, and using a good management system with the Lego kits. (My experience has been that students like this so much that they respect and follow our Lego management rules.)

Lego learning has been a major influence in improving the hands-on physical science learning in our classroom. I have included two exhibits to give you a sense of their potential and influence on children's learning. Figure 6.2 is a student response to a Lego/Logo activity. Figure 6.3 is the Lego/Logo rationale for its use (condensed from the Lego/Logo teacher's guide).

### Telecommunications

#### Description
*Telecommunications* is sending and receiving information over a long distance from computer to computer through telephone wires (electronic

**FIGURE 6.2** *Writing a Narrative* **Outline**

*Writing a Narrative* is a computer program that helps students develop an outline for writing a narrative. This example was generated after a student had answered a series of questions designed to organize student thoughts for writing a narrative. (Student responses are in capital letters and the computer-generated text format is in lower case.)

LEGO EXPERIENCE is the experience you chose to write about.
Your experience began TWO MONTHS AGO AT SCHOOL.
Here is what you have so far for your characters:
    KELLY
    MARY
    EVA
    JENNY
Here is what you have so far for your plot:
    BUILT STOPLIGHT
    BUILT ENGINE-POWERED CAR
    BUILT CHECK-OUT LINE
    BUILT GROCERY STORE BAG CART
    BUILT MERRY-GO-ROUND
Main objects in your experience:
    LEGOS
    BATTERY PACKS
    WIRES
    COMPUTERS
What was said or done that was particularly important:
    WE LEARNED MANY THINGS FROM EXPERIMENTING.
Feelings you had during this experience:
    PROUD
    EXCITED

**FIGURE 6.3    What Do Students Learn?**

1. Lego/Logo allows students to learn about computers, including the fundamentals of programming and how computers are used in the world. It involves the computer in learning ideas from many disciplines.
2. It encourages students to be scientists as they study science, which means they initiate the work, experiment and revise plans. Students exercise problem-solving and critical-thinking skills as they deal with both the concepts and process of science.
3. Projects incorporate math skills, such as measurement and fractions, and social studies material, such as invention and transportation.
4. Students learn personal skills of collaboration and teamwork as they work together on projects.
5. Students individually acquire self-confidence, which can spark an enthusiasm for school that may not have existed before.

mail). Basically, the equipment you need to telecommunicate is a computer, a modem, and a telephone line with similar equipment on the other end.

### How It Is Used

Telcommunicating has many different uses in educational settings and is expanding at a rapid pace. Telecommunications offers an affordable and quick way to exchange information on a global basis. It opens up the "information highway" that will no doubt replace some of the more traditional instructional materials. A primary consideration is the cost of telecommuncations. To get started, try a sample run by telecommunicating with a friend, a local library, or your students, or use E-mail with another school in the district so there is no online cost.

To get a taste of the possibilities with telecommunications, consider these four uses:

1. Telecommunications is a new way to communicate with other teachers or students. Teachers within the same building or in distant countries can reach each other via E-mail. Students can become pen-pals with their counterparts elsewhere in the world, and in doing so they bolster their reading and writing skills and awareness of other communities.

2. Bulletin board services (BBS), which usually are organized around a common theme or interest, are multiplying rapidly. An educators' bulletin board service would allow you to ask questions, leave messages, receive answers, and download files or shareware.

3. There are packaged telecommunication programs for educational use. For example, a school can purchase *National Geographic* software, study the topic, and then telecommunicate with other participating groups.

4. Internet, a worldwide telecommunications program, allows access not only to E-mail and bulletin boards but also to research databases.

### Examples

My class began using the *Hello!* software package from *National Geographic Kids' Network*. It introduces students to the telecommunications network concept and to scientific investigations. (See the disk included with this book for details about this program package and other *National Geographic* telecommunications packages.) Using the *Hello!* network, our class works with other classes around the world as a scientific research team, exploring the relationship between where students live and the kinds of pets they own.

We first used the *Hello!* software package as a whole group where everyone participated in all the activities. However, to have all students participate in all the activities was difficult to manage. Therefore, the next year, I designated one of the multisubject stations to be a *Hello!* station, where each station group was responsible for carrying out one activity. For example, Group #2 would work on Activity #2, Describing Our Community. Next, after adding the final touches to word-processing their community descriptions, they then go online to send their finished products to other participating schools. This approach proved much more efficient.

In their second year, students develop a greater understanding of telecommunications and learn to troubleshoot by using the *National Geographic Hotline Network.* Only second-year students use the hotline.

When we are not online, we continue to use the graphing and map-making features of this program for both project and learning-station work. We also discuss what this kind of communication means in our lives. Our second telecommunications package program, called *What Are You Eating?* also puts us in contact with other classes from around the world during a six-week session.

### Problem-Solving Software

In Rochester, Minnesota, a group of teachers devised what they call a Problem-Solving Skills Matrix. It divides problem-solving into four categories: memory, cognitive skills, strategies, and creativity. I use this matrix to reflect the broad definition I give to problem-solving software. Frequently, I include computer programs that offer drill-and-practice exercises (skill building) as well as software designed for building knowledge in this broad definition. A description of each software program is included on the disk that accompanies this book.

Some of the core problem-solving software I use are: Logo, HyperCard, word processing, database, and spreadsheets. Other software programs I have found useful are: *Type to Learn, Type, Quotient Quest, Spellevator, Wally Word Works, Writing a Narrative, Pond, King's Rules, Sim City, Where in the U.S.A. Is Carmen San Diego? Where in Time Is Carmen San Diego? Insects, The Rain Forest, McDraw, Dazzle Draw, Print Shop, Bank Street School Filer,* and *Write On!* There are many other similar software programs that may be equally effective. The important point is finding software that works in your curriculum.

### Integrated Learning Systems

#### Description

An *integrated learning system* is commercially developed hardware and software packages that offer student management options and lessons for individual use through a computer network. However, it can be run on a stand-alone computer. To fully utilize the system, training is necessary and is usually provided by the company.

### *Laser Disk Players*

#### *Description*

The laser disk player has a laser/optical device that reads images with the use of a laser beam. An audiovisual (AV) monitor is necessary to display the images. This technology allows a large amount of information to be stored on a 12-inch videodisc. This type of disc has the advantage of greater durability because it is not damaged by dust, fingerprints, humidity, or aging. Another advantage of these discs, except for the constant linear velocity (CLV) videodisc format, is that you can access each frame instantly rather than relying on fast-forwarding or rewind functions.

There are three different levels of interactivity for videodiscs and two types of videodisc formats. Each videodisc mentioned below is fully interactive, which means that it provides correction and immediate feedback on student responses. It also has branching features, which allow the teacher (or sometimes the student) to adjust the amount and type of practice to fit the student's performance. Students can freeze a frame to gather further information and self-pace their learning. These discs have strong oral and visual communication features as well as clear demonstrations. The discs are multisensory.

Here, too, I have found it wise to start small. Nothing is as easy as it looks and it takes time to learn about it and decide what is best for you and your students.

#### *How It Is Used*

Primarily, videodiscs are used to build students' knowledge base and to provide opportunities for practicing skills just as a textbook would do. Other uses are for student research, student presentation projects, or teacher-led instruction. Here are two examples:

- A World War II research project might include importing to the computer videodisc frames showing concentration camps.
- For introducing a book talk, a student can import a frame with an appropriate image by punching the frame numbers into the keypad. This is a nice feature for introducing a book talk because it can bring the viewer an image of the actual setting.

There are a couple practical matters to consider. Before doing any importing or printing of videodisc frames, check very carefully into copyright laws. Also, because neither I nor the students import or print frames regularly, it helps to post the steps, possibly with diagrams, near the laser disk player or production center. The expertise of second-year students is useful for these technical cord hook-ups. They like the responsibility and special recognition that comes from tapping their expertise.

#### *Examples*

***Weather and Energy*** Two science interactive videodiscs that I use are courses on weather and energy. Each course comes with videodiscs, a student booklet, a teacher's guide, and evaluation instruments. A key advantage of videodisc courses is that the narration is displayed on a screen as it is spoken, allowing a slow reader to concentrate on the content and comprehension rather than struggling to decode unfamiliar words.

These courses adapt well to a learning station, whole-group learning, or as independent work. If students miss a lesson, they usually make it up during choice time as independent work. We conduct the first two lessons as a whole group to introduce procedures for using the student book, software, hardware, and the individual lessons. By the third lesson, students are ready to use the course at a small-group learning station. They practice social skills of shared decision making and cooperation, by giving each person the opportunity to use the remote control and to choose a response.

The individual student booklet activities reinforce disc instruction. Because of the interactive nature of the videodisc, students have the option of "branching back" to hear the information again if they aren't able to answer a question from either the booklet or from the videodisc. Students practice proper grammar, neat handwriting, and drawing skills in answering booklet questions. Students are always free to access a frame to check for correct spelling, check for the correct answer, or facilitate a brief discussion with a neighbor.

I check student progress in three ways: by monitoring progress in the student booklet, by using the tests provided with the course materials, and by having students submit a short essay on what they have learned from the lesson. I do not use all three assessment methods for each lesson.

**Mastering Fractions**    Another videodisc set that I use is *Mastering Fractions*. These three double-sided videodiscs are fully interactive. I have used the *Mastering Fractions* program for several years and I believe it to be one of the best direct instruction methods for teaching students to understand every aspect of fractions. If you have never operated a laser disk player or used videodiscs before, the instructor's manual is very precise and elementary in walking you through the steps to proficient use of this program. The four major program features are:

1. Students are taught specific strategies for working various types of fraction exercises.
2. During each lesson, more than one skill is taught or reviewed.
3. Concepts are continuously and cumulatively reviewed.
4. The amount of prompting students receive for each concept or skill diminishes progressively.

Before we use *Mastering Fractions*, I introduce the first-year students to technical terms contained in the instructor's manual. I ask second-year students to be leaders at the manipulative station while we introduce the *Mastering Fractions* discs.

Some students developed a way to increase participation. They taped a transparency to the monitor screen and took turns having "a teacher" write the responses. Students know that if they use these discs and access certain chapters or frames to review, they will master fractions. The discs have quite a positive reputation, and rightly so. These sets of videodiscs are a tremendous help in permitting me to have more time for small-group work and discussion.

***BioSci II Elementary Edition***   This is a videodisc image database for biological science. This kind of videodisc used alone has limited utility unless repurposed (lining up frames in sequential order) for presentations and reports or used in a multimedia context.

## CD-ROM Players

### Description

CD-ROM disks are plastic, 4.72 inches in diameter, and can store a variety of media: text, graphics video, and audio. The capacity of a CD-ROM disk is over 650 MB (250,000 pages of text) as compared to floppy disks that hold .72 MB (360 pages of text).

A CD-ROM system needs a computer, a CD-ROM drive, a CD-ROM disk, and some type of speaker for audio output. CD-ROM capabilities can be stand-alone or networked; however, not every CD-ROM application can be used on a network. Some computers have an internal CD-ROM drive that also can be used to play regular CDs.

### How It Is Used

CD-ROM technology is rapidly changing the way we store and access information. CD-ROM disks include some of the following current applications: databases, interactive books in many content areas, games, music, catalogs, clip art, and encyclopedias. A single CD-ROM disk can store an entire 20-volume encyclopedia.

CD-ROM disk use is growing in our classroom. Most often, I introduce students to CD-ROM disks by following the training outlined in the section "Training the Students" in Chapter 2.

### Examples

I will discuss general uses of three CD-ROM disks: Grolier's *Multimedia Encyclopedia, The Coral Kingdom,* and *Bravo Books.*

In the past, locating the information was the most time-consuming part of doing research. Technology has simplified research. CD-ROM disks such as *Grolier's Multimedia Encyclopedia* provide instant access to information that can be updated easily. (A word of caution: Especially when students use the encyclopedia for research, the teacher must take an active role in guiding them to prevent electronic plagiarism [cutting and pasting electronic text] in creating reports.) Students use the electronic encyclopedia at the "How's it going?" station with teacher-directed instruction. This is followed by guidance and feedback during the research/writing process.

Students also use CD-ROM disks that contain encyclopedias and large databases for multimedia project work and for expanding their knowledge base. For example, a student selects, for her independent monthly report, the topic of the Great Depression. She finds information about the Depression Era using *Grolier's Multimedia Encyclopedia* and uses another CD-ROM disk to capture a video sequence from the Depression Era. The videoclip becomes a part of her report to the class.

*The Coral Kingdom*, an interactive CD-ROM disk, gives students an opportunity to master important concepts in environmental science, to learn ecological principles, and to explore a sea-life database. The program content is thematically organized into four major learning units:

1. The Discovering Adaptations unit introduces the theme of structure matching function and presents an overview of the diversity of sizes, shapes, colors, and behaviors found on a coral reef.

2. Coral Reef Ecosystem explores the formation of reefs and the vertical distribution of organisms on the reef face.

3. Investigating Interrelationships examines the ways organisms interact with the environment, explaining competition for food and habitat as well as symbiotic relationships.

4. Exploring Human Impacts addresses reef preservation and the impact of the development of the fishing and diving industries.

*A Mission* is a multimedia activity that students use to continue exploring *The Coral Kingdom*. Students work on each mission's specific objectives while at a learning station (usually the multimedia station). The structure of *Mission* makes it an effective way for students to start CD-ROM use successfully.

*Bravo Books*, a set of interactive CD-ROM disks, includes a storyteller feature that allows students to hear the story read from beginning to end with or without music, animations, and video. Any unfamiliar words are pronounced when the students click on them with the mouse. A multimedia glossary lets students explore the different *Bravo Books*.

The teacher and the students can customize the use of the book to fit the individual student's learning needs. For example, some students may need the story read slowly, word by word or by sentences, or it may be helpful to omit the narration of the story. *Bravo Books* can be a learning station activity, where the small group can work together on story notes, write about a favorite story part, or summarize a story.

These CD-ROM disks are only a few examples of the many CD-ROM disks available.

### Camcorders

#### Description

Most schools have a camcorder available for use in classrooms. Because it is fairly simple to operate, students become quite proficient very quickly. Recording requires a basic understanding of camera operations and accessories.

### How It Is Used

In a wide range of situations, the camcorder offers these important qualities:

- *Authenticity*: The camcorder is able to document and objectively record learning for purposes of review, assessment, and progress checks at a later date.

- *Visual history*: The camcorder provides a visual time line of a child's learning continuum.

- *Teaching tool*: The camcorder can be used to demonstrate a model of quality work and correct procedures, to present information.

- *Small-group-paced learning*: The camcorder tape can be stopped or replayed to allow for questions, for further information, or for clarification.

At the beginning of the year, ask parents and guardians if they will sign a form called "Permission to Videotape My Child and Play Back for Educational Purposes."

### Examples

Each of the following examples incorporate one or two of the camcorder uses.

1. Capture the expertise of a learning enhancement teacher or guest speaker. For example, when a traffic accident analyst spoke to six students in a learning enhancement class, we recorded his talk so that others could learn how his work relates to math and physical science concepts.

2. Preserve station work for later evaluation. Most of the time, students work on their own, putting together a three-minute video-tape production at the "broadcast news" station. At a later date, the students and I will view the videotape for the purposes of assessment and enjoyment. This is usually done at the "How's it going?" station.

3. In a student-to-teacher book conference, the student has four minutes to share a book he or she has read. This book conference is videotaped for the student to share with his or her family or for students to view as a choice activity. The book conference also is used for assessment purposes by the student and myself. The same process is used for taping Junior Great Book discussions. Periodically repeating this process provides an effective discussion skills progress check for both the students and myself.

4. A good example of high-tech/high-touch and multiple technologies working together is when we videotaped the construction of a playhouse in our classroom. Half of the class worked with a community volunteer to make the first playhouse, and we captured the volunteer's expertise and guidance on videotape for the

benefit of the other half of the class. They would make a second playhouse, which would be sold in a class fund-raiser raffle. Eventually, students realized they also could use the video to stimulate raffle ticket sales if they showed it while they were selling tickets. Computer technology skills were also incorporated into this project when students designed and printed raffle tickets on the computer.

The videotape for our annual wood-stenciling project also shows the value of video. Volunteers and students can refer to the five stenciling steps on the videotape before and during project work. It frees me to monitor the actual stenciling process, and it makes for a much more pleasant project-making experience when students have a resource other than the teacher. The camcorder is a valuable resource in helping you teach, especially with "how-to" projects that require precision and more individual guidance to help students produce high-quality products.

5. Students produce a videotape for other students to review and use as a way to assess both presentation skills and content understanding. For example, one year I asked the second-year students to plan a five-minute videotape on how to make an assignment notebook. In the videotape, students discussed the training involved in using the assignment notebook successfully; listed responsibilities for students, parents, and teacher concerning the assignment notebook; and listed the consequences for improper use of the assignment notebook.

6. The videotape is also effective for recording a chronology of students' oral presentations. Once a month, a parent will videotape each member of the whole class. Having just one parent do this on a regular basis works best. Some videotaping examples are:

   • Each student reciting a poem from memory

   • Each student reading his or her own story from the most recent published class book

   • Each student sharing his or her independent monthly project

The camcorder is the technology of choice for any task that requires direct instruction, clear demonstrations, or frequent repetition of instructions. I have made short teaching videotapes for most of the math projects so we can run the stations while conducting manipulative and problem-solving projects. Recently, second-year students have begun making short teaching tapes on specific math concepts.

### Examples of Videotapes

How to make a birdfeeder

Learning about a ruler

Learning about measuring cups and spoons

Presentation criteria and sample presentations

How to stencil on wood

How to set up your assignment notebook and use it

Notebook organization

## Videocassette Recorders/Players

### Description

The videocassette recorder/player (VCR) is available in most schools for classroom use and is such a common technology that it needs no explanation here.

### How It Is Used

The most frequent classroom uses are for knowledge building, gaining information, guidance for hands-on projects (such as making a birdfeeder), and assessment. Students usually view videotapes twice, once in a whole-group setting and then at a learning station. However, for hands-on projects, students may sometimes view it again, independently, to see specific parts they need help on.

## Audiotape Cassette Players/Recorders

### Description

The audiotape cassette player/recorder is still a valuable resource in the classroom.

### How It Is Used

I use the audiotape player primarily as a knowledge-building tool. For example, students at a learning station learn about different cultures when they listen to the *Keepers of the Earth* tape. The tape player also can be used in these ways:

- As a learning aid to assist the reader with decoding words, usually in an independent or small-group activity. When the children hear the words and follow along on the pages, they are able to enjoy and comprehend more from a book.

- As an accountability aid at a learning station when no adult is available, to verify that students read all instructions such as reading cooking instructions.

- As an assessment tool to record one-minute children's readings from a book for the teacher to listen to at a later time.

- To expand children's exposure to a wide range of music culture. In my classroom, I play a variety of music, from classical to popular, while children arrive and during their work on morning maintenance skills.

### Multimedia

#### Description

*Multimedia* is combining more than one media type for dissemination of information. Teachers have been doing this for years (an overhead projector and filmstrip used together could be classified as multimedia). Initially, today's multimedia tools appear to be more complicated to combine. However, let's take the example of using a computer with an internal microphone and an internal CD-ROM disk player. It means putting a CD-ROM disk into the disk caddy and then inserting it like a computer disk into the CD-ROM drive slot. Combining CD-ROM disks with computer software for teaching a concept is easier and less cumbersome than multimedia of years past. The equipment is more compact and accessible.

#### How It Is Used

The uses in the classroom should be determined by instructional need and not by the bells and whistles of the multimedia tool. The involvement of students in the production of multimedia presentations has the potential of increasing their learning immensely. No matter what the tool, its effectiveness is largely dependent on your knowing the potential capabilities and then knowing *how* to use it in light of availability, learning support, guidance, and accountability.

*HyperCard* and *Linkway* are examples of both *multimedia* and *hypermedia* (delivering information through multiple connected pathways). A hypermedia development program such as *HyperCard* allows students to branch seamlessly between text, graphics, audio, and video. For the rest of this discussion, I will refer specifically to *HyperCard*, which is computer software that is used to look for and store information—words, pictures, digitized photographs—about any subject. This information is stored in memory called stacks that are made up of cards. Each computer screen is called a card. Each card can contain a variety of objects, including fields (where text is stored and displayed) buttons (designated areas on the card that can initiate an action, such as branching to another card), and graphics (which can be created with *HyperCard* or imported from a clip-art program).

## TIPS AND TECHNIQUES

Keep in mind the following suggestions:

1. As with beginning station use, you can choose a starting point for technology by asking what subject is most comfortable for you or the area that you think you would be able to apply technology to produce a successful experience for yourself. For example, with the laser disk player, I started with an interactive science disk because I felt the need to build students' knowledge base so they

could get more out of Lego/Logo learning. The high-touch of Legos balanced the high-tech of the interactive science videodisc.

2. When allotting time on equipment, you may question how you can be fair and equitable with technology use. My definition of fair is that everyone gets what he or she needs rather than the *same* or *equal* time on the computer.

3. Some questions to ask yourself:

> What can the computer do for you?
>
> What do you want technology to do?
>
> What learning outcomes do you want?
>
> How can you understand what it will do for you or how it will help you?

4. Because the use of technology in the classroom is rather recent, teachers must develop a feel for when its use is appropriate. How can you tell when technology is facilitating learning? When it is functioning well, technology becomes nearly invisible. It blends in with the other learning tools and has an invigorating effect on the whole learning environment. When everything is working in the classroom and all students are busy with learning at all levels, you are creating a positive learning culture.

# chapter

## 7

# The High-Touch Process

What drew me to small-group, high-touch learning? Zoned-out looks, boredom, and the attitude of "Tell me what to do, when to do it, when to stop and, oh, how long does it have to be?" I was tired of giving the traveling evil eye to control students' behavior, dealing with short attention spans, and not really knowing my students on an individual basis. Most students didn't know how to persevere, figure something out, or experience the taste of success. I wanted active learners and good decision makers.

It became clear that the bridge I was crossing was of the same nature Nancie Atwell wrote about in *Coming to Know*, when she said, "We need to put the emphasis where it belongs: on meaning—and show students *how* to investigate to form questions and to communicate their findings, how to go beyond plagiarism to genuine expertise and a 'coming to know.'" This kind of learning can be achieved by exercising wisdom and perception in balancing both high-tech and high-touch in the learning process.

This chapter examines more learning activities that continue the *how* process of building skills and competencies, especially the foundation skills (basic skills, thinking skills, and personal qualities); however, the primary focus is demonstrating the high-touch process in children's learning.

Using a high-touch process in learning generates an atmosphere of shared growth, diversity, individuality, and working harmony. *High-touch*, then, is teaching to the whole child— responding to the child's social, emotional, and physical well-being as well as his or her intellectual abilities.

If high-technology is to become the tool, high-touch must become the process that renders the tool most effective. High-tech allows the teacher the time to give the personal touch—for example, to help students develop higher-level thinking skills in communication. Teacher Kathy Juarez puts it this way: "It's naive to think that even with technology kids are going to be able to make meaning of this incredible glut of information without learning to make connections between things, ask the right questions, make logical selections." (*Horace*, published by Coalition of Essential Schools, Vol. 10, No. 3, January 1994.)

## QUALITIES OF A LEARNING ENVIRONMENT

In his book, *Learning All the Time,* Jonathon Holt recalls being asked the following question regarding students' learning environment: "What sorts of things might we do to make various aspects of the world more accessible, interesting and transparent to children?" Holt's response was, "We must set up the learning environment to include time, freedom, leisure, and lack of pressure." When there is a relaxed, comfortable atmosphere, students and teachers alike are more able to do their best work.

## DEVELOPING THE HIGH-TOUCH LEARNING ENVIRONMENT

The following are some techniques that I have found useful for developing the high-touch learning environment:

- *The process stays flexible and child centered.* The activities that I share with you in this chapter can happen freely and can meander like a river, with the children usually determining the course. The way the activities are used gives them the high-touch feature so needed alongside technology.

- *Students make choices with consistent, careful guidance from the teacher.* Activities designed to offer choice give students many opportunities to practice handling freedom responsibly. Thus, students develop competence in self-management, self-confidence, and self-assessment. Cultivating these skills is a slow but rewarding process.

- *Old-fashioned hard work and accountability are the finishing touches that affect the process and the product.* As the teacher follows up on expectations, students learn to meet obligations and form good work habits. The teacher serves as a model for discussion and also provides guidance and feedback as students develop questioning techniques, share, listen to others' ideas, and build discussion skills.

Creating this environment calls for experimentation and teamwork as students and parents join the teacher in rethinking, retraining, and reflecting about the learning environment. The ultimate criterion is that the environment allows activities to take on a high-touch quality.

## ACTIVITIES

This chapter will explain activities that generally take place outside the learning-station framework. The following is a list of these activities:

Reading and writing block (including Junior Great Books, fables and literature/discussion books, and writer's workshop)

M & M Skills

Homework Packet

Class Meetings

Choice Time

*NewsCurrents* Filmstrips

Entrepreneurship

Parent Night

Learning Enhancements

Goal-setting Conferences

Each of these activities is described, and an example is given to show how it is used. While reading about these activities, you will see how students are immersed in reading, writing, speaking, and listening. You will also see how these activities integrate guidance and feedback from the teacher, volunteers, peers, and technologies to produce high-quality learning. All the activities are designed to help build self-esteem and social skills, to provide opportunities for making choices and to meet quality standards, and to give the teacher ample time to care for children while helping them do their best.

## READING AND WRITING BLOCK

Developing students' reading and writing competencies is one of the major focal points in education. The previous chapters have illustrated that the learning-station format is a powerful, practicing environment for advancing these competencies. In this chapter, I demonstrate how these skills—reading and writing—are incorporated into other learning activities in our classroom. This resembles a whole language literacy model.

Downsized groups, technology, and volunteers allow me to put this whole language theory into effective practice. In part, whole language is about teachers and students making decisions together. It is about setting up a learning environment that is purposeful, authentic, and based on both the children's and teacher's desire to know. Choice and ownership are two aspects of the whole language philosophy that, when carried out effectively, produce an important by-product: self-esteem. Decisions and choices based on careful evaluation, reasoning, and sound judgment don't just happen. Teachers and students have to cultivate these skills together. This takes time.

As I follow the basic theory and practices of whole language, integrated reading and writing become the heart of the curriculum in my classroom. We devote considerable time to literature and writing, integrating it throughout the curriculum. However, we also have a specific reading and writing block where the emphasis is on reading good literature (and lots of it) and developing a writer's voice, using Donald Graves' *Writer's Workshop* philosophy and techniques.

My journey has taken me from a reading curriculum where the basal reader was the primary tool to one that incorporates more approachable materials, such as paperbacks and magazines, that helps students make connections with their world. The basal, once the core of the reading program, is now used as a classroom reference book to enhance other content areas. This wider range of materials means there are more opportunities to interest readers. Consider Ellen's story:

> About the third week of school, students were signing up to begin reading their first literature book. Ellen hadn't signed out a book. So, during the day I met with her and asked which book she was going to read. Her response was, "I don't like to read." Together, we looked through the four books she could select from: *Black Beauty, Call of the Wild, Call It Courage,* and *Bridge to Teribithia.* I knew she would like a thin book, and maybe *Bridge to Teribithia* could be the book for her.
>
> If I think a child can handle it, I usually challenge him or her to read 10 to 30 pages in one evening, depending on the child's reading and confidence level. Ellen exceeded the original challenge that night and finished the book in three days.
>
> A year later, Ellen's mother thanked me for working with her and then laughed as she explained that she always has a book in her hand now, but she has to draw the line when they go out to eat.

A student reaches one mountain top when he or she gets excited about reading. That individual reaches another when he or she discovers the relationship between reading and writing. Therefore, one of the many high-touch strategies is to introduce good literature to students, which also serves as a vehicle for building students' knowledge base in content areas.

In the book *Invitations,* Regie Routman states that a balanced reading and writing program includes opportunities for:

Reading and writing aloud

Shared reading and writing

Guided reading and writing

Independent reading and writing

I like to include these opportunities through specific reading activities such as weekly fables, Junior Great Books, daily oral reading by the teacher, literature/discussion books, book conferences, book database, learning stations, and optional activities. All of these activities involve a variety of group sizes, from whole-group to small-station groups to pairs or individuals. Because of time restraints, it is impossible to do all of the following activities every year, but I include them here to illustrate the range of reading activity options.

## Fables

### Description
Every other year, we use Aesop's fables. Each child receives a fable book. Every Monday, a different student selects a new fable for the whole class to read. There is a weekly fable quiz. To remind students of the weekly fable title, students chose to write the fable title on the cover sheet of their homework packet and to post a note with the fable title above the classroom light switch.

### How It Is Used
Students are required to read the fable twice independently during the week. To create additional learning opportunities, I ask students to compile the quizzes into individual booklets where they can eventually see cumulative progress in:

1. Meeting fable quiz standards
2. Handwriting
3. Critical thinking, such as interpreting the meaning of the moral and relating it to life today
4. Spelling (When words are misspelled in the quiz, students are expected to write them correctly in the section of their spelling notebook called "Words I Need to Work On.")

### Recordkeeping and Storage of Fable Quiz
There are two different fable quiz options for students. See Figures 7.1 and 7.2. As a group, the students decide which to use first, and then we switch to the other quiz in a couple of months. Usually, we review each person's first quiz at the "How's it going?" station by using the fable quiz criteria. I store fable quiz forms on a computer file, and I use a spreadsheet to record the students' quiz results.

**FIGURE 7.1  Aesop's Fable Quiz 1**

1. What is the fable title?

   _____

2. Write out the moral.

   _____

   _____

3. Name two characters.

   _____

   _____

4. What does the moral mean to you and how does it relate or apply to your life?

   _____

   _____

   _____

### *Junior Great Books*

#### *Description*

Reading literature is a meeting of minds between author and reader. Junior Great Books is designed to teach children in grades 2 through 12 how to interpret what they read. The main elements of Junior Great Books are excellent literature and a method of discussion called *shared inquiry*. The selections range from classic folk tales and modern short stories to the works of great thinkers. Required training for Junior Great Books leaders is provided by the Junior Great Books foundation. Some related advice on discussion leadership can be found in Figure 7.3. (Also see Figure 4.3 in Chapter 4.)

I have developed the following discussion questions and guide shown in Figure 7.3 from the Great Book Foundation and the Paideia Foundation resource materials.

**FIGURE 7.2   Aesop's Fable Quiz 2**

1. What is the fable title?

_____

2. Write out the moral.

_____

_____

3. Name two characters.

_____

_____

4. Illustrate the fable.

**FIGURE 7.3   Techniques for Expanding Questioning**

- "Why do you say that?"
- "What do you mean by that word?"
  (slave or servant—How are they different?)
- Point to a word; "What does that word mean?"
- Refer to a specific word in a text; "How does that fit?"
- Have the students defend their position; "How do you support that from the text?"
- If you think that they are incorrect in their use of a word, ask: "Why do you use that word?" "Is that the author's intent?" Use a similar word (i.e., servant/employee): "Does it fit?"
- If they are going too fast, slow them down with "I don't quite follow you."
- If they are puzzled, ask: "What puzzles you?" "Look for a specific word." "Read the text that puzzles you."
- Involve other students in a response: "What do you think about . . .?" "Do you agree with that?"
- When an answer is muddled, look for the reason; ask about it. Repeat the point to the student. Use the basic concept again in a question.

### How It Is Used

I introduce the whole group to Junior Great Books in a brief teacher-led instruction and then show an introductory Junior Great Books videotape that presents the philosophy, how it works, and a few examples of Junior Great Books discussions. Students get a better understanding of both the teacher's and students' roles when they see students like themselves engaged in actual discussions.

### Additional Training

The week before students make their first story selection, I design a multipurpose station—using a parent to review four posters (available through the Junior Great Books program). These posters address:

1. Notetaking

2. Follow-up questions

3. Using the dictionary

4. Discussion techniques

Generally, second-year students don't have to attend this station. However, I will ask a second-year student to go to the station if I believe he or she needs the review. One of the details explained at this station is how students use 3-inch by 5-inch, lined, sticky-back note paper to jot down thoughts about the book, then place it inside the front cover and use it for reference during discussion. Reading the story twice and having the note paper in place are requirements for Junior Great Books to participate in a discussion.

### Forming Discussion Groups

When beginning Junior Great Books, either the students or I select two stories and enter both titles on a word-processing file. During one afternoon, everyone takes a turn signing up for the story they wish to read. We now have our two groups, with approximately half the class for each group. Each group meets for discussion twice each month. The following factors seem to yield high-quality discussions:

1. The mix of first-year students and second-year students

2. The smallness of the group

3. Students remaining in the same discussion group for about three months

Having everyone participate might mean making adaptations, such as arranging for an audiotape or finding time to help a student who is learning disabled read the story. With an audiotape, the slow reader can both hear and see the words; the multisensory approach helps the student read the story and builds his or her self-confidence. It has been my experience that ability levels disappear in the discussions.

*Assessment*

For assessment and evaluation purposes, I videotape discussions. Videotaping the first couple of discussions helps groups assess and improve discussion skills. The students and I critique them together, either at a learning station or in a whole group. Repeating this process periodically provides an effective check of discussion skills.

---

**FIGURE 7.4    Junior Great Books Seating Chart**

Notes for the discussion leader (this is an "open book" discussion):

> Why do you think . . .?
> Is it relevant?
> What makes you think . . .?
> Do you need evidence?
> What in the story . . .?
> Is it clear?
> Afraid of what?
> How can . . .?
> Can you explain?
> Do you agree or disagree?
> Return to the opening discussion question.

This seat chart was designed by one of my students.

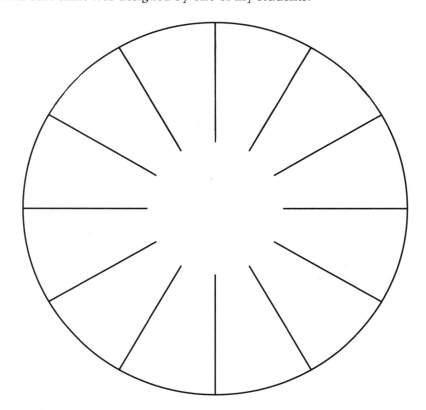

During the discussion, I use a seating chart to record students' comments next to their names. Reflecting on these comments is helpful for follow-up questions and assessment purposes. See Figure 7.4 for a sample of the seating chart that I have adapted for Junior Great Books discussions.

If you have access to a laptop computer, this is a perfect time to use it. With a laptop, you can enter students' comments quickly and legibly, and you can make additional notes pertaining to each story. Other advantages are easy access to notes stored on the hard drive and an easy method for chronicling student comments. It is also an opportunity to model a practical use for a laptop versus a standard computer.

### Rewards

Junior Great Books gives you an opportunity to see discussion skills blossom. Students are able to listen and respond to someone else's statement. They speak when it is appropriate without raising their hands or asking the teacher's permission.

## Oral Reading

### Description

As a part of the high-touch process, I read aloud to the whole class for 20 minutes almost daily, using a variety of reading materials, including different kinds of books, newspapers, magazines, and recipes.

### How It Is Used

I use oral reading time as an opportunity for students to practice listening skills, enjoy literature, expand their reading interests, and relax. While I'm reading to students, they may also use their sketch books for drawing about the reading or use prepared drawing exercises from the book, *Drawing with Children,* by Mona Brooks.

In one instance, I read the book, *My Brother Sam Is Dead,* to introduce students to our social studies topic: the Revolutionary War era. The fictional story helped to build the students' awareness and interest in the topic. During this time, students could jot down any word, term, place, or name that was new or interesting to them in their social studies notebooks. I invited students to share their notes. This reading and sharing grew to be quite a high-interest activity, so we started a computer file on the book where one person periodically entered all the information shared by the students. We repeat this process when appropriate.

I also use oral reading time to introduce activities that may be explored in greater depth at a learning station or in other learning activities. For example, I use the *Draw-and-Tell* book by Richard Thompson, which is an excellent tool for teaching storytelling techniques. It provides an innovative way for students to learn about the structure and pattern of a story and to develop their storytelling ability. Later, students can choose this book as one of their independent weekly activities (which will be discussed later in this chapter). The students like to work in pairs, with

**FIGURE 7.5    Mystery Picture from *Uncle Bob* Story**

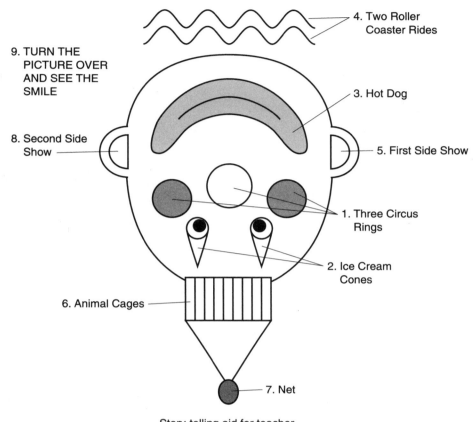

Story-telling aid for teacher.

*Source:* Richard Thompson, *Draw and Tell* (Willowdale, Ontario: Annick Press, 1988). Reprinted with permission.

one child telling the story while the other draws the mystery picture. See Figures 7.5 and 7.6.

### Literature/Discussion Books

#### Description
I use many different types of literature, both nonfiction and fiction. Some of the categories include historical fiction, adventure, mysteries, biographies, and autobiographies.

#### How It Is Used
The finish date is usually four to five weeks. I use a whole language approach, varying the literature based practices and activities according to our overall theme, area of study, time, volunteer availability, and number of books we are using.

**FIGURE 7.6   Mystery Picture from *Uncle Bob* Story**

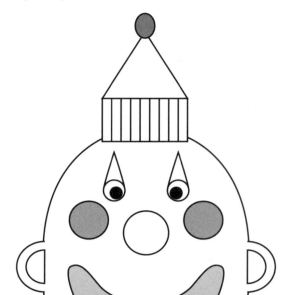

This is the drawing turned over.

*Source:* Richard Thompson, *Draw and Tell* (Willowdale, Ontario: Annick Press, 1988). Reprinted with permission.

Technology plays a significant part in many of the discussion book activities. It may be as simple as using a word-processing program to compose a summary of each chapter. Other times, we may use computer software to create an animated script of a book presentation or *HyperCard* to create a book review.

I use discussion books to develop students' enjoyment of reading, to build reading and comprehension skills, and to obtain or expand new interests and knowledge. Also, these books provide good writing models for students and the chance for students to make the connection between writing, reading, and thinking.

For one segment, I might select four books with an animal theme emphasizing the underlying themes of courage, integrity, friendship, self-esteem, caring, and loyalty. I post the four book titles with a brief description of each book and put out a copy of each book for students to see. Next, the students sign up for one book. Each book group meets to determine how many pages they will read by their next meeting time. It is not unusual for students to finish a 250-page discussion book before the agreed-upon finish date.

## Book Conferences

### Description
The student and I sit down and visit for approximately four or five minutes about the book he or she has read. Another student videotapes this conference. The conference can be based on any book the student has read.

### How It Is Used
I use this as an opportunity for students to speak and have one-on-one time with me. It is a very comfortable setting, designed to build the speaker's self-confidence. The objective is to develop an articulate discussion about a book, rather than use the traditional interrogation with "canned" questions (Who is the author? Who are the main characters? etc.). Also, this is a way for me to learn more about an individual student's book interests.

## Book Database

### Description
Students set up a database and enter the information about their book according to the different database fields. (See Chapter 6 for further details.)

### How It Is Used
This activity gives students practice using a database and understanding how it works. It serves as a resource for all the students. For example, if a child is interested in mysteries and wants to see other titles, he or she can type in the word *mysteries* and call up all the mystery titles that others in the class have read. (This database can be used for extended reading and math activities.)

## Integrated Writing

Regie Routman's words state my beliefs about writing: "I believe that literature provides the best models of language. Through reading, thinking about, discussing and interpreting great literature, students come to learn most of what they need to know about language — especially if the teacher takes the time to note the demonstrations the literature provides (for example, the leads, the conventions, the vocabulary)" (From *Invitations: Changing as Teachers and Learners K–12*). Routman quotes Frank Smith's article, "Reading Like a Writer," when she adds this insight: "The way to become a writer is through becoming an insightful reader."

Reading teaches about writing, and writing sets more learning in motion. For example, writing about a topic—that is, conducting research and absorbing new information—requires more thinking and learning than simply reading about it. Whether writing on a blackboard, on a computer, or with online telecommunications, students must learn how to use words to communicate effectively.

### Examples

The foundation of my writing theory and practice is derived mostly from the book, *Writing: Teachers and Children at Work* by Donald Graves. Graves presents a writing workshop process that is thorough, easy to understand, and easy to implement. Best of all, it works. I have added computer power to the workshop using word processing and *Write On!*— computer software that functions with word processing and focuses on process-writing skills. *Write On!* is flexible enough for the teacher to tailor the lessons to fit specific writing needs of individual students. (See the disk included with this book for further details about *Write On!*). The purpose here is not to discuss in detail the *how* of the workshop technique, because Donald Graves has already done that very effectively. I mention Graves' book here because it is such a valuable resource for teaching the writing process.

Using Graves's technique, students develop competence in everyday writing tasks. These tasks may involve writing information for themselves or for others in the classroom, such as writing meeting agendas, notetaking, class newsletters (comic, cartoon, and editorial writing), class messages, script writing, and anecdotal assessment comments.

### Writing That Meets Special Needs

A child who has learning disabilities learned to use the word processor to write a story. After participating in a writing conference with me, he shared his story at the Author's Chair (where students read their original work to the class). The biggest reward for me was observing his determination and confidence in accessing his word-processing file and getting his story ready for publication.

## Communications Outside the Classroom

Our class regularly uses writing and speaking skills for ordinary tasks such as composing permission slips, guest speaker invitations, and scripts for telephone calls. For all these speaking and writing tasks, I am the final editor, managing quality control, helping with spelling and punctuation, and listening to the scripts.

These communication tasks are voluntary efforts by the students, and the frequency of these tasks allow everyone to be involved. Therefore, it is not necessary for everyone to do the same task at the same time, such as writing 30 thank-you notes to one person. This is a different mindset, but it works. The enthusiasm to do the work is high because the students have most often chosen the task and take pride in being responsible for the job. The following are some examples of the tasks the students have done:

### Examples of Communications

1. We need more parent drivers for the learning enhancement pottery class. A few students write the notice to be sent home with all the students.

2. A few students write a note to community volunteers who have helped with a building project in our classroom. In this note, they thank the volunteers for their help and invite them to have lunch with us in the classroom.

3. Two students call the bus garage to arrange class transportation to the pizza place.

4. Students learn how to leave a message on voice mail when they call a software company for technical assistance.

5. Two students call to get prices on pizzas. They present the pizza price information to the class and the class chooses one by voting.

## MORNING MAINTENANCE SKILLS

### Description

My students begin arriving at school 15 to 20 minutes before school officially starts. As a class, the students decided to begin work right away when they come into the classroom. Students use this time to work on morning maintenance (M & M) skills, which focus on basic skills. The students select one of three types of M & M skills to work on: follow-up lessons; person, place, word, and quote; or independent weekly activities. Students use the selected type of M & M skill three days a week for a three-month period and then select a different type. Descriptions of the M & M skills are discussed here.

### Follow-Up Lessons

Follow-up lessons can be about strengthening weak spots in punctuation, grammar, capitalization, geography, or math. This usually deals with weaknesses detected through my observations or conversations with students. It is a chance for the teacher to follow up on specific learning needs. (See Figure 7.7 for a Sample Follow-Up Lesson.)

### Person, Place, Word, and Quote of the Day

Students practice research skills and expand their world knowledge by getting information about a person, place, word, and quote of the day. Usually, I select the items in this activity to relate to current news or to a particular area of study. Students take turns at submitting a person, place, word, and quote of the day also. This helps me and the other students to

FIGURE 7.7   Sample Follow-Up Lesson

# This Week

1. _____
   _____

**T**uesday   2. _____
   _____

3. _____   4._____

1. _____
   _____

**W**ednesday   2. _____
   _____

3. _____   4._____

1. _____
   _____

**T**hursday   2. _____
   _____

3. _____   4._____

learn about each student's interests. Students enjoy reciting the quotations from memory. (See Figure 7.8 for samples of person, place, word, and quote of the day.)

### Independent Weekly Activity

Students may select 1 to 3 activities from a group of 10. A printout lists all the different activities for that week. Individual activity sheets or work material hang on a vertical clothesline for student selection. Students contribute activity ideas and share with me the task of checking off an

### FIGURE 7.8    Person, Place, Word, and Quote of the Day

### Week One

Name _____ Date _____

PERSON—Ralph Waldo Emerson _____

PLACE—Concord, Mass. _____

WORD—quality (bonus—essence) _____

QUOTE—Self-trust is the essence of heroism. _____

_____

_____

PERSON— _____

PLACE— _____

WORD— _____

QUOTE— _____

_____

_____

PERSON— _____

PLACE— _____

WORD— _____

QUOTE— _____

_____

_____

**FIGURE 7.9   Independent Weekly Activities**

Choose one to three activities.

- Memorize a poem of 10 lines or more.
- Memorize four prefix definitions and list two words using each prefix.
- Select an invention/inventor to report on from inventions book.
- Complete dictionary skills sheet.
- Fill in states on a U.S. map.
- Fill in country changes on a map of Africa.
- Select a country and tell me the language, religion, economics, and other key facts from the "Where in the World" cards.
- Complete one exercise from basic parts of speech software.
- Select an art project— for example, origami.
- Memorize eight lines from "Punctuation Rap."
- Read and tell me about a short article of interest to you from *Cobblestone, Zillions,* or *Adventures* magazines.

activity when it is completed. Later, these data are entered into the appropriate spreadsheet either by myself, a parent, or a couple of students. (See Figure 7.9 for a list of possible independent weekly activities.)

### Turning Lost Time into Bonus Learning Time

As a means of getting students interested in using this morning time and realizing its cumulative value, everyone takes part in figuring out the extra learning time we are getting in a week, month, and year. Without M & M skills, there would be, on the average, 45 minutes of time lost each week, three hours each month.

## HOMEWORK PACKET

### Description

The multidisciplinary, weekly homework packet allows students to practice basic skills, connect their learning to the world around them, and apply their knowledge. Activities include worksheets that support classroom learning (English, math, and geography skills), outside reading (*3-2-1 Contact, Zillions,* or *Cobblestone* magazines, newspaper), educational programs on television (*Square One* or *Where in the World Is Carmen San Diego?*), and hands-on experiential learning (making a colonial saltbox house model according to written instructions.)

Each homework packet has a cover sheet that serves as an assessment record and a work history that students and I can review. The cover sheet has several helpful features, including some that were the result of student suggestions. (See Figure 7.10 for a sample of the homework packet cover sheet. This is also on the disk included with the book.)

**FIGURE 7.10   Homework Packet Cover Sheet**

| Homework<br>Due Friday, January 14 | Total Points |
|---|---|

**Tasks are challenge level and are optional (choice).

Name _____   Work Partner _____
Parent Signature _____   Time Spent on Homework _____
Parent or Student Comments:

| Math/Problem Solving | Points |
|---|---|

| Language Arts | Points |
|---|---|

| World Awareness | Points |
|---|---|

| Choice Reading | Points |
|---|---|

| Other | Points |
|---|---|

*Class Notes/Reminders:

### Noteworthy Features of the Cover Sheet

- *Student record of the amount of time spent on the packet.* This helps the student establish a history of time spent on the homework packet, and it serves as a gauge for me to see if the average length of time to do a homework packet is staying within the projected two-hour completion time.

- *Parent's signature.* Extra points are given for the parent's signature. This is a way of encouraging parent involvement, and it helps the teacher to ensure that the packet has been checked for quality and completeness.

- *Special notes section.* This space allows for extra communication from the parent or the student.

- *Work partner section.* Students have the option of working with a partner, either a family member or a classmate (outside of class). If they do, they list the person's name here.

- *Challenge work section.* I include at least one optional challenge activity that is indicated with stars (**) in front of the activity title. When a student works on a challenge activity, I record a star on the spreadsheet.

### How It Is Used

The homework packet is sent home with students at the beginning of the week and is due back on Friday. Every Monday afternoon, I use the whole-group setting to go over directions on the cover sheet and other pages of the packet. It is important for the teacher to read the directions to the students and to ask the students questions pertaining to the cover page to determine their understanding of the tasks.

Parent involvement is encouraged as parents help their child complete parts of the packet and supervise the time allocated to do the homework. When parents are involved, they become more aware of special interests their child may have and areas of weakness that need additional support. They also can share with me incidents—sometimes comical and delightful—about that week's homework packet. This gives me further insight into each child and how the homework packet is going.

### Content

I design the packet using a variety of skills, worksheets (teachers have abundant amounts of these), reading materials (book assignments or short magazine articles), and hands-on activities that may be a combination of learning activities. Learning activities correlate with current classroom learning or serve as readiness activities for future learning or review.

I try to introduce the students to quality children's television programs through the homework packet. I also incorporate a reading selection that students can read to a family member, so that they will view reading as a family activity.

### Assembly

Each student assembles his or her homework packet every Monday, using an assembly-line model. The students move to the packet-making area according to table groups during the time I read to them. Sometimes I run a contest, rewarding the class with a special bonus for assembling the packet accurately and in record time. It is helpful to videotape the process in the beginning and then again a month or two later. Students can view the tape and assess their assembly work using questions such as these: Is there a particular table group that has exemplary behavior? Has the time been cut? How efficient is the overall process?

Students are responsible for assembling their own packet. They know the consequences for sloppy assembly work, such as missing a page. This method teaches responsibility and consequences, and it saves me time.

### Quality and Responsibility

Homework packets encourage students to work for quality and be responsible for planning their time so that packet work is thorough, complete, and neat. At the beginning of the year, students learn the standards set for the different parts of the packet and strategies for meeting those standards. They learn how to use the cover sheet as an organizational tool.

### Turning in Homework Packets

Each Friday, students must place their packets in a basket and check off their name on a nearby spreadsheet *prior* to the Pledge of Allegiance (the official start of the day).

If a student returns a homework packet that is not complete or is of inadequate quality, the consequences are that I meet with them to discuss the problem and how to remedy it. After the review, the homework packet is sent home with a note to parents requesting their help to review the work and to see that it is done well. The parents are asked to sign the note. The same process is used with late homework packets. I have found that once students thoroughly understand the meaning of quality work and accountability, they seldom need further correction on these issues. I keep a record of the number of late homework packets for each student. Students are involved in determining the consequences for being late with their packets—for example, working on their homework packet during choice time.

### *Recordkeeping*

I use an electronic spreadsheet to record homework packet results. Each section of the homework packet is evaluated by using either points or comments (superior, excellent, satisfactory, redo, or sometimes an anecdotal comment). The spreadsheet indicates whether a packet had to be redone or was late. Sometimes, volunteers enter the homework packet results.

Correcting the homework packets is time consuming, and most of the time I correct them myself. In the first couple of weeks that students use the homework packet, we review corrected packets page by page at the "How's it going?" station so students can see how each part is evaluated and voice their questions. The objective is to train for quality and thoroughness.

### *Storage of Homework Packet*

I keep the following homework packet information in both my filing cabinet (hard copy) and on my computer disk: (1) cover sheet format and (2) cover sheets filed by date. I also keep a hard copy of each complete homework packet. A future development I can see is to create a topic and skills homework packet database for cross-referencing.

### *Everyone Likes It*

Students generally like the packet idea. Their comments indicate that they appreciate:

1. The freedom in planning when to do homework
2. The chance to make decisions about work options
3. The cover page, especially checking off when work is completed
4. The variety of audiences they can read to (someone on the bus, someone older, someone younger, a favorite stuffed animal)
5. The variety of reading materials

Students love the diversity and innovation demonstrated by the contents of the homework packet. It also gets them thinking imaginatively, and soon they submit fantastic learning ideas. Some ideas aren't workable, but students nonetheless show they have the right attitude—that learning can happen any place and that there is no limit for creativity and thinking about learning.

Parents seem to like the homework packet because they can play a role in shaping it. I improve it by using ideas or acting on comments that they have submitted. They also appreciate the routine of the homework packet and the manageability of the booklet form versus single sheets on a sporadic basis.

I like the homework packet because I do not waste time hassling students about daily assignments. The packet puts into practice many of the SCANS skills and competencies, and the notes/reminders section of the cover sheet is a convenient vehicle for communicating with parents.

## CLASS MEETINGS

### Description

A 10-minute meeting is usually planned at the end of each day to take care of any unfinished business and to plan for the next day.

### How It Is Used

The meetings are used to check the learning pulse. How did we do today? Where do we start tomorrow? Students can write thoughts on a comment board throughout the day. At the end of the day, I check the comment board to see what needs to be discussed at this short meeting. Also, because I know that I am very task oriented, I like to use this time, especially in the beginning of the school year, for students to voice concerns or to ask questions that I may have overlooked or may not have had time to address to a student's satisfaction.

For instance, one student shares that there is just too much to do sometimes in class. Another student shares that she writes down everything she has to do and then decides what to do first, second, and third. I use the meeting to reinforce the idea that we are in this together, and that everyone needs to communicate their ideas and comments—whether positive or negative—so we can all do a better job. I find that children love to hear other children's solutions to problems.

Every two weeks, we have a large meeting where I compile every issue or coming event that I need to talk over with the students. Originally, I posted a Meeting Concerns sheet a few days before the large meeting so students could jot down items they wanted discussed. It wasn't very successful. However, after a suggestion from a student, we developed a computer file called "Class Meeting" and everyone (students and I) enters items as they arise. During the meeting, we display the file on the large monitor and highlight the item we are discussing. Some students like to have a printout of the meeting items as well, so they can more easily follow along. These meetings can be conducted in a whole-group setting or with half of the class at a time.

At the beginning of the year, I explain to the students how the class meeting works. I then ask the question, "What is the value of having you enter meeting concerns before the time of the meeting?" The usual response is, "So we don't forget." However this year, a second-year student said, "It means if we think it out first when we write it on the computer, students are more prepared to explain their thoughts at the meeting."

The original reason for the daily comment board (11 × 18 page) was so that we could write a weekly newsletter more quickly and more accurately to report on the week's happenings. Each day, we would have a new comment page, about 12 inches by 18 inches. In the beginning, I modeled, reminded, and coached students to write on the comment board. Eventually, they wrote comments on their own, and I continued to do so too. Besides using the comment board for gathering current issues for meetings, it also helps students tell their parents about something *specific* they did in school.

## CHOICE TIME

### Description

Choice time is a group activity where students choose either to work together or individually on whatever interests them most. Choice time lasts approximately 30 minutes and occurs two to three times a week, usually at the end of the day. This activity is designed to expand the students' range of incidental or exposure learning options while fostering student decision making and student-relevant learning.

### How It Is Used

This is a sampling of activities you might find students engaged in during a typical choice time:

- Writing a skit for a book presentation
- Building on a Lego project
- Finishing a floorplan model
- Using any computer, CD-ROM, or videodisc software (I rotate the software)
- Reviewing "Broadcast News" videos.
- Playing educational games, such as *World Traveler, Where in the World, Authors,* checkers, chess, Monopoly, puzzles, Pictionary, Good Old Houses (a puzzle game of historic American architecture), and *Go Build* (matching architects with their buildings)

Another valuable activity for choice time is a book titled *I Know That Building!* which includes activities and games to help students discover architecture. Students sometimes bring games and models from home to share for choice time.

Educational games and Lego building are the favorite choice activities. Students enjoy it when the teacher or parent volunteer participates in a small group. This is also a time when I can visit briefly with a student or two to show further interest in students as individuals and engage in conversation. It is also a time to show students I like to play, maybe even win. It presents a perfect opportunity for subtly helping students refine grammar skills and social skills. For example an often-heard question while playing a game is, "Do you got...?," to which I respond, "No, I do not *have*...."

This is also a time that students practice good social skills. They share games and usually display care and respect for each other. Students remember to include the person who may not have someone to play with, and it is not uncommon for me to hear students offer the game they have been using when they see a classmate who wants it.

### Storage of Choice Materials

Most of the materials are stored in a box that was constructed to serve as a bench as well. It is packed with fun. Children love to peer into the box, deciding which game to pull out. I rotate the games on a regular basis to expand their interests. It is all about making connections, exposing them to more information about their world, and sometimes creating new interests or pursuits of learning.

Students take the responsibility of putting away any items they used during choice time. Periodically, the helper of the day does an overall check to see that all materials are put away neatly. Students are required to put away their materials within the last five minutes of choice time. In the beginning, I may use the large monitor or a piece of covered cardboard to display a variety of activities for choice time. After a couple of weeks, students take to this activity quite nicely without any additional suggestions.

## NEWSCURRENTS *FILMSTRIPS*

### Description

*NewsCurrents* is the title of a weekly current events and news filmstrip and discussion guide that present world news. The discussion guide supplies information and questions for each filmstrip frame and can be used to initiate group discussion, which promotes interactive learning. The guide contains three levels of script (basic, general, and advanced), making it appropriate for grades 3 through 12. (See further details about *NewsCurrents* on the disk included with this book.)

### How It Is Used

At the beginning of the year, students vote on whether to view the filmstrip with half the class or in a whole-group setting. My students always choose the half-group configuration, which encourages discussion and enhances the learning experience. The groups, divided according to their Junior Great Books clusters, each have 45 minutes for viewing and discussion. The students and I take turns reading from the guide, discussing the news, learning about people and places we sometimes haven't heard of before, and sharing experiences and views on many issues. When the entire class has seen the filmstrip, students take the short multiple-choice and essay quiz provided in the discussion guide.

Other examples of how I use this filmstrip are:

1. At a learning station, for the purpose of more in-depth learning on one of the major topics in the filmstrip

2. As a learning resource for research work (second-year students can create a *NewsCurrents* topics database for easier access)

3. As a background visual for presentations; for example, the students used the filmstrip frame of the "information highway" as a background visual in their presentation

## ENTREPRENEURSHIP

### Description

Students in my class ran a decorative can business for five years. The "tin art" creations were made by punching holes to make a design, such as a flower, on a one-gallon can. (See Figure 7.11 for an illustration of the tin art flower design.) The business demonstrated the value of parent involvement, because the idea for the tin art came from a parent.

### How It Is Used

Parent volunteers and I organized the business during its first year, and it proved to be one of the best ways to build a sense of community. Students were eager to help make and market the product. They did all the advertising and sales work. The work of preparing and making the cans took place either at home or after school.

As the business grew, students learned more about starting a business, organizing, and management, and, most important of all, marketing. Students became very familiar with basic terms such as *materials cost, profit, labor cost, losses, assembly line, advertising, precision, neatness, quality work,* and *product.* The longer we were in business, the more innovative the students had to become about how and where to sell the cans.

At first, students sold to their parents and friends. Next, their "tin art" was sold at school conferences, at a local restaurant owned by a student's parents, and in the cafeteria at lunchtime. Finally, their creations were sold at a local craft fair. Students increased the number of designs customers could choose from and created compact design order booklets (all-

**FIGURE 7.11    Tin Art Flower Design**

occasion and Christmas). They used a computer to develop order forms, electronic spreadsheets, and charts to monitor inventory, costs, and profits. Written materials were submitted to me for final editing before using with the public.

We came up with the decorative can project in order to raise transportation money for field trips, and we succeeded in meeting all the financial goals. There were two additional reasons for this project: First, I think it is very important that students learn how to earn money; second, I value the sense of community that naturally develops when you are working together toward a common goal. Working with a hand-made product had its advantages. Hand-made creations are very special, and when students sell these items, they know everything about them. The practical experience students gained through this business proved to be one of the best kinds of learning they could have had.

### *Marketing Skills*

Students developed skills in maintaining customer interest and sales. The following are a few examples of their ideas, which include a poster presentation, a surprise can, and a compact order booklet:

- *Poster Presentation:* One student's poster advertised the many different uses for these cans.

- *Surprise Can:* Students filled one can with jelly beans, and the first person to purchase the can with a design matching the filled can would get the jelly beans. While the Surprise Can was in use, sales increased by about 25 percent.

- *Compact Order Booklet:* Students created this booklet to make it easier for customers to choose a design when we didn't have a decorative can available.

### Integrating Part of the Business into the Curriculum

In the third year of the decorative can business, we included a can-making station in the art and culture learning-station plans about once a month. A volunteer would assist at this station.

### Skills Used Chart

Students learned new skills through the decorative can business by:

- Projecting a budget for the field trips
- Planning how to use the profits
- Organizing and replenishing the patterns for the cans
- Producing quality cans
- Visiting a bank to open a checking account
- Keeping an accurate inventory of raw materials and finished products
- Keeping accurate sales records at the problem-solving station
- Deciding how much to charge and when to run a sale
- Deciding how much to cut the price in order to increase sales but to maximize the profit
- How to set prices for damaged cans
- Producing clearly written instructions for "How to Make Decorative Cans" (the result of a request from a parent who thought this would be a nice family activity)
- Explaining the decorative can project to visitors
- Using communication skills when selling the cans
- Designing the sales/ordering booklets
- Designing the order form
- Practicing safety

### Ramifications of This Business

The decorative can business had some unexpected results, including these:

- The business spawned a healthy classroom atmosphere, encouraging students to practice good relationships and helpfulness with each other and their customers.

- There was increased interest in entrepreneurship, so we offered a class called "Starting Your Own Business" as one of the learning enhancement choices. I taught the class using the Busine$ Kit, an elementary approach to entrepreneuring. Kids explored business organization and marketing, and they took a field trip to a bank to gather information on bank services to businesses. Two students started businesses after this class.

We answered requests for instructions on making decorative cans from homemakers clubs, craft clubs, Girl Scouts, and 4-H groups. We later thought this may have affected our sales. Once the market appeared to be saturated, we began looking for a new business product.

## PARENT NIGHT

### Description

Parent Night is a key opportunity for students to get additional presentation experience. This is a program in which students show parents, grandparents, brothers, sisters, and others what they have learned, using various forms of presentation. This is a real community-building activity and an example of high-touch involvement. The smallest attendence for any of our programs was 72 visitors. This kind of attendance is an indication that people enjoy these programs. Students are enthusiastic as well. In one case, a boy walked a mile just to be there, even though his parents had to work.

Overall, Parent Night is a festive occasion. Families are invited to bring refreshments and they certainly do. We have wonderful parties at the end of each program.

### How the Program Evolved

Initially, I began doing Parent Night simply for students to have the experience of a program performance. Each year, we have changed the format in the following areas:

1. We have gone from, first, the concept of performance, progressing to an exhibition of our work-in-progress, to audience participation in re-creating our learning environment and culture. Now, we don't prepare a play or songfest but rather fine-tune a station plan in preparation for the program. In this way, we present what we are learning in the classroom and the parents gain an intimate knowledge of what their children do during the day. The visitors participate in the station plan activities.

2. We have gone from using teacher content plans to shared *teacher/ student* planning for the program. This whole process becomes a valuable learning experience for everyone. Some considerations are:

   What do we want to accomplish?

   What format would work best?

   Can we pull it off considering the number of people attending?

3. We have gone from *my* designing the program agenda sheet to *students* putting together a program agenda sheet. We usually do this at a learning station with the help of a parent volunteer.

4. We have gone from individual parents videotaping the program to a volunteer videotaping the program to be shared with all of the parents. We also use the tape later in the classroom for both assessment and enjoyment. Therefore, the tapes become an effective learning tool as well as a valued keepsake.

5. We have gone from *my* being the program moderator to having *students* take over the microphone.

When we finally accomplished the goal of audience participation, we also created an atmosphere in which the visitors could enjoy themselves, stay relaxed, and have meaningful conversations with students and other visitors. Students shared information with parents to facilitate their taking part in learning-station work. From these experiences, parents gain insight and get a taste of the in-depth learning inherent in these activities. What is exciting about parent night is that it mirrors the actual high-touch learning-station culture—that is, learning in an atmosphere of enjoyment, relaxation, and meaningful conversations.

The amount of student involvement in planning, organization, and orchestration is phenomenal (again, however, I am the final quality-control manager). We lay out the general outline for the program at a whole-group meeting and then go into specific details at my learning station. Later, I designate at least two of the multisubject stations for program rehearsal. A parent volunteer and I assist at the rehearsal stations, and in this way the work stays very manageable. Second-year students have learned from their first-year program experience, and they are very helpful at orchestrating this venture with me.

## LEARNING ENHANCEMENTS

### Description

Learning enhancements are another important component of the high-touch classroom. These are small-group classes taught by the teacher, parents, professionals, artists, high school students, and community members with specific areas of expertise.

Learning enhancements originated because of my strong belief that the community has many learning opportunities to offer children. I use learning enhancement classes to extend or enhance students' learning in specific subject areas and to expose students to topics in which they have expressed an interest. Also, parent involvement grows as they help design some of the classes.

Learning enhancement classes are offered three to four times a year. They usually take place once a week over a four-week period. Each class is approximately one and a half hours. Usually a field trip is incorporated into each of these classes.

The variety of classes offered at any one time will vary according to topics, space, supplies, and teacher availability. Most often, there are four topic choices offered.

### How It Is Used

In one instance, a lawyer teaches a class entitled "The Constitution and You," which involves examining a few constitutional cases through role-playing and taking a field trip to a federal or county courtroom to hear a case being tried. After the field trip, students demonstrate what they have learned about the Constitution and how it relates to them by producing a videotape role-playing a court case.

It is amazing how many mentors and teachers from the community are available and willing to help out in the classroom. High school language students frequently offer introductory lessons in a foreign language. Students enjoy getting to know these young adults and getting a taste of which language they might like to study in future years.

### Number of Learning Enhancement Classes

I usually select the number of classes to be offered, taking into consideration the following: subject of class, volunteer and building space availability, and student preferences. Some factors to consider in arranging for the class selections are (1) whether volunteers are comfortable with a large or small group of students; (2) whether it is an activity (such as weaving) that requires one-on-one instruction; and (3) whether instructors prefer to work with a large group of students (a local potter wanted to instruct all 13 fifth-graders in the class in order to make the most of her time investment).

### Other Considerations

The commitment to open the classroom to community volunteers requires the classroom teacher to use clear communication skills and to act as the main contact with the learning enhancement volunteers. By initially talking with the volunteer, the teacher can get a feeling for how well the volunteer will relate to the students and how many students he or she can handle. For each new learning enhancement teacher, I supply a form that requests an outline of his or her plans so I can review it ahead of time. Time spent planning the scope and activities of each learning enhancement class is key to having successful and enjoyable learning experiences for everyone.

Volunteers also can be grouped in a teaching team. For example, a group of two or three high school students might plan and carry out a language class. This allows backup in case one of these presenters has a conflict and can't be there for a class session. A community volunteer with special expertise, such as gardening, can be joined by a parent volunteer who can help students with hands-on activities.

### Sign-Up, Transportation, and Student Skills

About two weeks before learning enhancement classes begin, students take home detailed descriptions of the classes, including field trip permission slips. The sign-up form, signed by the parent, is returned after students have checked their first and second class choices. Parents are sometimes asked to provide transportation for a learning enhancement class to reduce cost. The teacher should be sure that drivers' automobile insurance covers liability for the number of students they transport.

Students choose their learning enhancement classes and work closely with the learning enhancement teacher, following the appropriate classroom expectations. The students also build interpersonal skills as they work with other members of their group and the "new" teacher. Because many of the classes have a cultural or societal focus (language classes or art), students are exposed to social systems from diverse areas.

### Costs Involved

Most learning enhancement classes are free. However, there may be times that you offer a special class that will cost a small amount. For example, a talented potter was asked to participate in learning enhancements. She was very busy producing saleable pottery for an upcoming show and mentioned that she would need to be reimbursed to justify taking time to teach the class. Consequently, each pottery class participant was asked to pay a small fee of $3.00. In addition, the potter was allowed to set up a display of her artwork in the lunchroom before one of the learning enhancement classes. She made enough money through sales to staff members, together with student fees, to make her visits worthwhile.

Sometimes, our class projects have generated enough money to cover incidental costs for these classes.

### Learning Enhancement Forms

Part of the successful organization of learning enhancement classes includes good communication with parents, students, and volunteers. I use several forms to facilitate this communication. The following are titles of the different learning enhancement forms I use. (Samples of these forms are included on the disk that accompanies this book.)

Letters Announcing Learning Enhancement Classes

Learning Enhancement Class Descriptions

Learning Enhancement Registration Forms

Learning Enhancement Planning Form

Field Trip Permission Forms

Learning Enhancement Evaluation Forms

## GOAL-SETTING CONFERENCES

### Description

Setting learning goals is also part of the high-touch process. When the child, parents, and teacher share in deciding the child's goals for the first semester, a sense of commitment and teamwork develops. Goal setting is used to guide and focus a child's energy toward learning growth. It is used as a planning tool that gives children more practice learning a real-life skill, and a by-product is improved self-esteem.

### How It Is Used

It is valuable to conduct the goal-setting conference a couple of weeks before school starts to reduce some of the beginning-of-the-year fear and anxiety. However, if this kind of time commitment is unrealistic, planning conferences for the first month of school works well also. The goal-setting form is filled out at the conference. We use the multiple intelligences identified by Howard Gardner. See Figure 7.12.

At the first conference, much of the time is spent explaining the concept of each "intelligence" category to the child and assisting them in setting goals. Because parents know their child best, they are a major influence in their child having a successful goal-setting conference. With each conference, the child becomes more vocal, reflecting on prior goals achieved and setting new goals. The children become more adept at developing an action plan to achieve these goals.

I enter everyone's completed goal-setting conference information onto a computer file titled according to the year and semester. Next, each student can transfer his or her individual conference information onto a file on the child's personal disk. The student, parents, and I each have a hard copy of the goal-setting conference information. To make these goals more meaningful, I request that students keep their goals sheet in a place that they look at frequently. On occasion, I have each child choose one of his or her goals to focus on for a while. He or she then writes the goal on an index card along with the steps involved in achieving this goal. This parallels the goal setting that students do in math. The philosophy is that in order to learn to do, one needs many opportunities to practice doing it.

---

### FIGURE 7.12   Goal-Setting Conference Form

#### Goal Setting: A Parent, Teacher, and Student Process

Student's Name _____ Grade ___ Teacher_____

Intrapersonal: self-confidence, responsibility, self-management...


Interpersonal: relationship with others, respect, solving problems, group work...


Linguistics: reading, writing, speaking...


Logical—mathematical: math, problem solving...


World—understanding: science, social studies...


Bodily-kinesthetic: physical education, dance, coordination...


Spatial: geometry, spatial reasoning, visual arts...


Musical: vocal, instrumental...


Other goals for your life beyond the classroom...


Signatures: student, parent, teacher...


Designed by Ms. Ellison, Barton School. Reprinted by permission.

---

## TIPS AND TECHNIQUES FOR THE HIGH-TOUCH PROCESS

- Take notes on your students, especially at the beginning of the year when meeting with them at a station. For example, one of the first activities that you take care of at the book-learning station is introducing math goals. While students are writing their math goals, you have an opportunity to see their handwriting, spelling, grammar, punctuation, and capitalization skills, as well as getting a general impression of their comfort and skill level in math. There are many ways to record this: take written notes, videotape, audiotape, or use a laptop computer.

- Meet in small groups and/or with half the class to observe each child. Study the children as they converse, paying particular attention to their individual characteristics.

- Use the camcorder to capture various learning situations.

- Become a "kidwatcher." What do the children appear to like? Are they patient? What is the diagnosis? Is a particular student's problem a lack of motivation, poor time management, or poor organizational skills?

- Keep questioning. Talk with the student and get answers. Develop a learning profile.

- Build a collegial and comfortable environment with your students.

- Participate in choice time. It builds that high-touch community spirit.

- Keep them listening, responding, talking, and making decisions.

- Set up the learning environment so everyone—you and your students—really has the opportunity to know each other.

- Follow up! Follow up! I always like to clarify in a humorous way that this isn't nagging or being mean. It is called caring enough to ensure each student's learning accountability. Using humor helps keep us all happy most of the time.

## CONCLUSION

Leaving the classroom has sharpened my vision. My leave to write this book was punctuated with weekly teaching duties. Those trips to the school confirmed what I was writing about and at the same time helped me see even better how much I had changed since the beginning of my journey. There is an applicable quote from R. S. Trapp: "It is difficult to see the picture when you are inside the frame." My journey isn't over, but I've come far enough to see the benchmarks of success. One student summed it up in a written evaluation of the class, when she reported, "We use a lot more thinking and problem solving than in a normal classroom."

This student underlined the next statement:

"<u>The program proves people wrong who say you can't be learning if you're having fun.</u>"

W. Edwards Deming, a noted economist, states, "Organizations must constantly improve themselves by focusing on customer satisfaction, employee education, doing things right the first time and involving people who are closest to the job at hand." Over the years, I have tried to incorporate these principles into the learning environment and have found that the best we can offer children is ourselves, by showing them we are life-long learners who are constantly rethinking, retraining, and reflecting as educational professionals.

Ann McFarland, a noted specialist in child development at the University of Pittsburgh, said, "We don't teach children. We just give them who we are and they catch that. Attitudes are caught, not taught. If you love something in front of a child, the child will catch that." So what is our attitude to be? I suggest we abide by Garrison Keillor's advice: "Be well, Do good work, and Keep in touch."

---

## AUTHOR'S NOTE

Although this book is based on actual experiences, it is not intended to single out any specific individual. I have changed all names to protect the rights of my students. If you, the reader, have any comments on the content of this book, I am anxious to hear your viewpoints. Please write to Ms. Joan Riedl, P.O. Box 191, Clear Lake, MN 55319.

# *Index*